D1593136

STALIN'S
SECRET WAR

STALIN'S
SECRET WAR

The NKVD on the
Eastern Front

RUPERT BUTLER

Pen & Sword
MILITARY

First published in Great Britain in 2010 by
Pen & Sword Military
An imprint of
Pen & Sword Books Ltd
47 Church Street
Barnsley
South Yorkshire
S70 2AS

ISBN 978 1 84884 053 9

A CIP catalogue record for this book is
available from the British Library

Typeset in Ehrhardt
by S L Menzies-Earl

Printed and bound in England by
CPI Antony Rowe, Chippenham, Wiltshire

Pen & Sword Books Ltd incorporates the imprints of
Pen & Sword Aviation, Pen & Sword Maritime,
Pen & Sword Military, Wharncliffe Local History, Pen & Sword Select,
Pen & Sword Military Classics, Leo Cooper, Remember When,
Seaforth Publishing and Frontline Publishing

For a complete list of Pen & Sword titles please contact
PEN & SWORD BOOKS LIMITED
47 Church Street, Barnsley, South Yorkshire, S70 2AS, England
E-mail: enquiries@pen-and-sword.co.uk
Website: www.pen-and-sword.co.uk

Contents

List of Plates

Acknowledgements

The author would like to thank Alfred A. Knopf, a division of Random House Inc., for permission to draw on *A Question of Honor, Forgotten Heroes of World War Two* by Lynne Olsen and Stanley Cloud, 2003, and *Imperium* by Ryszard Kapuscinski (translation copyright 1994 by Klara Glowczewska).

Little, Brown & Company gave me permission to draw on *Special Tasks (Revised)* (copyright 1994, 1995) by Pavel A. Sudaplatov and Anatoli Sudaplatov, Jerrold L. Schecter and Leona P. Schecter.

Particular thanks are due to Professor Chris Bellamy, Professor of Military Science at Cranfield University and to Professor Donald Rayfield, Professor of Russian and Georgian at Queen Mary College (University of London), for guiding me to several valuable NKVD sources.

The author would also like to thank Dr Frank Ellis for permission to quote from his article '10th Rifle Division of International Troops NKVD: Profile and Combat Performance at Stalingrad', *The Journal of Slavonic Studies*, Vol.19, No.3, September 2006, pp.601–8.

Simon Zaremba recalled for me his experiences while fighting in the Polish partisans and his role in Operation Feston. My thanks also to Jeffrey Bines for giving me permission to quote from his privately printed account of the operation.

Zianon Pazniak and Yauhen Shmyhaliou gave permission for the use of material from their June 1988 article 'Kurapaty: The Road of Death' which appeared in the Belorussian newspaper *The Literature and the Art*.

Lech Kwasibororski kindly let me draw on his account of the arrest in Poland by the NKVD of his mother Bronislawa and her subsequent exile.

Thanks are also due to Dr Andrzej Suchcitz, Keeper of Archives, The Polish Institute and Sikorski Museum, London, for providing valuable background on the Katyn Massacre and the activities of the Home Army.

Gustav Rust was particularly helpful in letting the author draw on his *'In the Clutches of the NKVD and the Stasi – Behind the Wall of Shame and Barbed Wire: A Documentation*', consisting of documentary evidence taken from NKVD/Stasi files, Polit-Verlag Gustav Rust, Berlin.

Leave to record the experiences of Vilnius Corporal Jozef Rodziewicz at the hands of the NKVD was given by the editor of *The Sarmatian Review* Vol. XVIII, No.2, April 1998. www.ceeol.com

Lev Mistetskiy's account of his service in western Ukraine is quoted with the permission of Centropa, the Vienna-based library of Jewish studies.

Grateful thanks are also due to John Montgomery of the Royal United Services Institute for Defence and Security Studies, to the London Library, the Institute of Contemporary History and Wiener Library and the Imperial War Museum. I am especially grateful for research and editorial assistance provided by John Crossland and Joyce Rackham.

A number of translations from the Polish were kindly provided by Jacek Skiba and Camilla Buczek.

Chapter 1

The Pursuit of Power

Nazi Germany's whirlwind invasion of the Soviet Union, Operation Barbarossa, broke in the early hours of Sunday 22 June 1941. A concentrated barrage of artillery was unleashed over the German–Russian front, stretching from the Baltic to the Black Sea. Three German air fleets spread chaos and confusion deep into the back areas, blasting airfields along with scores of grounded Soviet aircraft.

German troops were camped short of the Bug river which, since September 1939, had been the German frontier with the Soviet Union. The river banks were silent save for the croaking of frogs. Then, at 3.15am, the hitherto silent, shadowy western horizon exploded into the thunder and lightning of artillery barrage, coming from 7,000 German guns. Frontier guards viewed a sky fractured with blinding flashes. As they stumbled from their barracks through the haze of smoke, they were greeted by the squeal and clatter and thud of mechanized armour.

At 3.25am, Josef Stalin was jerked from his sleep by Chief of General Staff Georgi Zhukov, the shoemaker's son who was to become one of the Soviet leader's most trusted aides and the eventual hero of the defence of Moscow. After serving as a cavalry NCO in the forces of the Tsar, Zhukov had climbed the career ladder fast. This was the man known as *Zhuk* ('the beetle'), who had all the coarseness and brutality of his peasant background and matched his leader in total lack of scruple when action was needed.

Zhukov told Stalin that Russia would face a war front over 2,000 miles long, against forces consisting of more than five million men: the German Wehrmacht buttressed by Italian, Hungarian and Finnish allies.

Stalin nominated himself Supreme Commander and Commissar, heading a State Committee of Defence of the Soviet Union. The ultimate aim was to gear his forces to fight the Germans in what became known as 'The Great Patriotic War'. The State Committee was made up of four members who, besides Stalin, were seasoned Politburo appointees: Kliment Voroshilov, Georgi Malenkov, Vyacheslav Molotov and Lavrenti Beria. The position of each of these men depended ultimately on the approval of a notoriously capricious leader.

Intimidation, Cruelty, Terror

As a dictator who was to rule his vast empire for three decades, Stalin's sole aim was to shape Russia's politics through the pursuit and exercise of power. Loyalty even to devoted colleagues meant nothing. Sentiment had no place. The survival of Josif Vissarionovich Dzhugashvili, born in Gori, Georgia, who had adopted the surname of Stalin ('steel') in 1912 when in his thirties, was assured by intimidation, cruelty and terror. He firmly believed that he was beset by enemies on all sides. Resentful, vengeful and carrying grievances for years, he had all the characteristics of paranoia, suspecting that plots and conspiracies were perpetually brewing around him, orchestrated by some group that was seeking to harm him. A lifetime role model was the Tsar Ivan the Terrible, from whom he adopted the policy of punishing not only those people he perceived to be his enemies, but also their extended families.

Stalin's daughter, Svetlana Alliluyeva, looking back on her father's career some years after his death, was to declare: 'He gave his name to this bloodbath of absolute dictatorship. He knew what he was doing. He was neither insane nor misled. With cold calculation he had cemented his own power, afraid of losing it more than anything else in the world.' Stalin's ability to witness cruelty without any emotion could, by his own admission, be traced to his childhood, when he witnessed a public hanging in the centre of Gori. Two men, pursued by mounted police, had shot one of the officers; the police had then dragged the other man to a gibbet and garrotted him. Many of Stalin's character traits could be traced to his brutal father,

Vissarion Ivanovich, whose ill-temper was inflamed by drink and who was said to have beaten both his wife, Keke, and their son. As a boy Stalin had endured ceaseless taunts about his appearance. At the age of seven he had contracted disfiguring smallpox, earning him taunts of 'pock'.

At the behest of his devout mother, Stalin trained for the priesthood in the Tiflis seminary, but was expelled in 1899 for rebelling against the church's authority. By then he was reading Marxist literature and devoting his time to the Georgian branch of the Social Democratic Party, which sought the overthrow of the Tsar and the introduction of socialism. Although not a major player in the Bolshevik seizure of power in 1917, he rose through the ranks of the party as a confederate of Vladimir Lenin, leader of the revolution and then head of the Soviet government. By 1922, Stalin had become General Secretary of the Communist Party. He was careful at first to keep a low profile, watching events and building a base for support.

When Lenin died on 21 January 1924, Stalin lost no time in pursuing power, adroitly removing likely rivals. Prominent among these was Leon Trotsky, a Jew and the leading figure of the Left opposition. One of Trotsky's chief disagreements with Stalin centred on his belief that socialism would not survive unless there was world revolution, while Stalin maintained that Russia could remain strong by her own unaided efforts, a belief termed 'Socialism In One Country'. As General Secretary, Stalin was able to summon sufficient support to edge Trotsky from his post as Commissioner for War, and in 1927 contrive his expulsion from the Party, followed by exile to Central Asia and later deportation from Russia.

Rise of Beria

It soon became apparent to close colleagues, many later to be victims of arrests, deportations and executions, that, on a mere whim, Stalin could send anyone's career into freefall. Especially aware of this was Lavrenti Beria, who was to hold a key appointment as early as December 1938: the post of controller of the Soviet Union's machinery of terror. This was the NKVD (*Narodnyy Komissariat Vnutrennikh Del*, the People's Commissariat of Internal Affairs).

Surviving accounts of Beria's appearance and character are virtually unanimous in declaring him evil-looking and physically repulsive. Here was a short, balding and fleshy individual with a thick and sensual lower lip, rotting teeth and penetrating snakelike eyes glistening behind professorial pince-nez. Many who worked with him later attested to his obsessive, fawning pursuit of personal advancement. The British journalist Edward Crankshaw described Beria's outward manner as 'gentle and coldly, abstractly benign – the whole effect of that pedantic aloofness which makes people think of scholars when they should really think of fanatics of the most dangerous kind.' This view was echoed by an American journalist, Craig Thompson, who pointed out that there were those who fell into the dangerous trap of assuming 'that Stalin had at last decided to put his cops in the charge of a history professor. The assumption only proved how little they knew.' Of Beria's inbred ruthlessness, a colleague attested: 'Beria is a man to whom it costs nothing to kill his best friend, if that best friend said something bad about Beria'.

Beria particularly impressed Nicholas Kviatashvili, a Georgian by birth, who was able to observe him closely at the Allied Tehran conference of 1943, noting: 'He seemed completely to disdain any opposing view, was quite intolerant of anybody else's opinions and became very angry if anyone strongly opposed any of his proposals. Not that any of the Soviets dared – they behaved like slaves in his presence.'

Lavrenti Pavlovich Beria, son of a peasant, had been born on 29 March 1899 in the hamlet of Merkheuli, within the Azerbaijan region of Georgia, formerly an independent principality under the patronage of the Tsarist empire. By the time he was a teenage student in Baku, the Bolshevik Party, proclaimed as the vanguard of the revolutionary proletariat under Lenin, had seized power during the Russian Revolution, sweeping away the Tsars and the house of Romanov. A rival group of revolutionaries, the social democratic Menshevik Party, had been ruthlessly suppressed in Georgia following invasion by the Russian Red Armies, after which Georgia became a Soviet republic. Throughout Russia, a rule of terror had come to control just about every aspect of political and social life, enforced by a relentless secret police, designed to root out traitorous elements and those who presented even a mild threat to security.

A secret police service was not new in Russian history. During the time of Tsar Alexis (1629–76), a highly efficient Bureau of Secret Affairs had been created to provide agents who penetrated the heart of the Duma (council of state), spying and reporting on military leaders and even foreign ambassadors. On his travels, Alexis was shadowed by bodyguards and agents, whose duties included penetrating a newly established foreign postal service. Correspondence from abroad was delivered first to the Foreign Office, where it was slit open and all worthwhile information acted upon.

By the time of the 1917 Russian Revolution, intelligence and espionage had passed to the Okhrana (*Otdeleniye po Okhraneniyu Obshchestvennoy Bezopasnosti i Poryadka*, the Department for Defence of Public Security and Order), an integral part of the Ministry of International Affairs of the Tsarist empire. It was responsible for, besides the security of the Tsar and the imperial family, opposition to organisations regarded as hostile, including socialists and would-be revolutionaries. All manner of underhand methods were developed, in particular covert operations by undercover agents, including police incursions into workers' groups, house arrests and the sifting of private correspondence. The Okhrana's methods survived the revolution, whose architects did not shy from adopting its methods.

The successor to the Okhrana was the All-Russian Extraordinary Commission for Combating Counter-Revolution and Sabotage (*Chrezvychainaya Komissiya po Borbe s Kontr Revolyutsiyei I Subotazhem*), otherwise known as Vecheka, the Cheka. At the behest of Lenin and his acolytes, house arrests by the Bolsheviks were stepped up to terror level. Small printing presses, where opposition parties had printed their one-sheet newspapers, were smashed. As a state security organisation, the Cheka served as a template for the future with its programme of repression, which came to be known as 'Red Terror'. An edition of *Krasnaya Gazeta*, the organ of the Red Army, outlined a lurid campaign: 'Without mercy, without sparing, we will kill our enemies in scores of hundreds. Let them be thousands, let them drown themselves in their own blood ... Let there be floods of blood of the bourgeoisie – more blood, as much as possible ...'.

The Cheka also had its own 'house journal', *The Red Sword*, which was edited by a devoted adherent, Martyn Latsis, a Latvian, who outlined what he saw as the organisation's main functions:

> The Cheka is not just an investigative organ: it is the battle organ of the party of the future... It annihilates without trial or isolates from society by imprisoning in concentration camps. Its word is law. The Cheka's work must cover all areas of public life... When interrogating, do not seek material evidence of the accused's words or deeds against Soviet power. The first question you must ask is: what class does he belong to, what education, upbringing, origin or profession does he have? These questions must determine the accused's fate. This is the sense and essence of red terror... It doesn't judge the enemy, it strikes him. It shows no mercy, but incinerates anyone who takes up arms on the other side of the barricades and who is of no use to us... But it isn't a guillotine cutting off heads at a tribunal's instance... We, like the Israelites, have to build the kingdom of the future under constant fear of enemy attack.

Lenin's desire to overthrow the established order through revolution could be traced back to his own early experience of the secret police. In May 1887, when he had been 17 years old, his eldest brother, Alexander, was arrested and hanged with others for involvement in a terrorist plot to kill Tsar Alexander III. Lenin appeared unfazed by Cheka killings. During an address in January 1920 to trade union leaders, he confessed: 'We did not hesitate to shoot thousands of people, and we shall not hesitate, and we shall save the country.'

Iron Felix

Lenin's most able lieutenant was the Pole, Felixs Edmundovich ('Iron Feliks') Dzerzhinsky, founder member of the Cheka and to Lenin 'the true Knight of the Proletariat'. Born in September 1877, his career as a revolutionary had begun when, at the age of 20, he had spurned further education and gone to work in the factories and slums of Vilnius as a Marxist agitator. Almost a total aesthetic, misleadingly softly spoken and with elegant manners, he had spent time in many Tsarist jails, where he had closely studied his interrogators, later applying their practices to his own Chekist prisoners. He and Lenin favoured merciless reprisals and slaughter in the face of even the smallest signs of opposition. When it came to controlling those who worked for him, he adopted methods that survived well into the Stalin era. He drove his subordinates hard and expected them to cope with a crippling workload. When they collapsed with exhaustion, he dismissed them instantly.

One event served as a handy pretext for rounding up opponents such as the splinter group, the Socialist Revolutionaries, former officers and those identified as members of the bourgeoisie, all of whom were destined to be shot without trial. On 31 August 1918, when in Moscow to address a meeting of factory workers, Lenin was fired on in the street and wounded. Fanya Kaplan, standing nearby, known to be a sympathiser with the Socialist Revolutionaries, was arrested as the chief suspect. Although her identity as the would-be assassin was never established precisely, she was condemned to death and shot by Pavel Malkov, the Kremlin commandant. Her body was stuffed into a steel oil drum and cremated.

The call for vengeance went on to become a major issue. In the following month, *Pravda* (Truth), a leading newspaper and an official organ of the Communist Party Central Committee, declared: 'The Bourgeoisie is an indefatigable enemy. The rule of capital will be extinguished only with the death of the *last* capitalist, the *last* landowner, priest and army officer.' Gleb Ivanov Bokii of the Petrograd Cheka reported to Moscow that 800 alleged revolutionaries had faced the firing squads, and another 6,299 had been imprisoned.

As a target, the bourgeoisie included just about any individual who displayed even the smallest signs of opposition. The measures adopted against them were to remain broadly unchanged as the Cheka became the NKVD and subsequently the KGB (*Komitet Gosudarstvennoy Bezopasnosti*, the Soviet Security and Intelligence Service). Across Russia the central state authority ruled with an iron fist. The regime exhibited the prime characteristic of most dictatorships: its precise powers were never cast in stone. Those who controlled it could do much as they liked. For instance, on 26 October 1917 Lenin issued a Decree on the Press, which gave him the power to close down any newspapers publishing material deemed to be hostile.

Another characteristic of the dictatorship was a power struggle within the Cheka, closely involving Josef Stalin, whose rate of promotion within the inner Bolshevik circle had proved sensational. By late 1917 he had secured the key post of Commissioner for the Russian Nationalities. Beria lost no time in joining the Cheka, where he secured the post of Chief of the Secret Operative Division, making sure that accounts of his own endeavours reached Stalin, who was to commend him for his 'Bolshevik ruthlessness' in putting down insurrections.

Figures vary as to just how many individuals had been executed by the Cheka throughout Russia, including Georgia, by 1920. The hard-line Bolshevik Martyn Latsis, the editor of *The Red Sword*, cited 12,733 between 1918 and 1920 as an official figure, but there is general agreement among later historians that this was a gross understatement and a figure of around 250,000 is now considered more likely.

As a result, the Cheka was so loathed and feared, even by the most loyal Bolsheviks, that Lenin became increasingly aware of the need for some semblance of revolutionary legality within the regime. He consequently approved a decision to close down the Cheka.

Its eventual successor was the GPU (*Gosudarstvennoye Politischeskoye*, the State Political Administration). Nominally the GPU answered to the Ministry of the Interior, and its responsibilities were officially restricted to the investigation of civic crime. The secret police, however, remained untouched, its members still being known as 'Chekists'. In the next year came yet another title: OGPU (*Obyedinennoye Gosudarstvennoye Politicheskoye Upikvlenie*, the Joint State Political Administration). An ongoing problem remained the activities of freebooters and criminals, who claimed to be former supporters of the Cheka. Police control across the whole of Russia became even more rigid.

However, in Moscow, the Soviet Union's epicentre, there was another preoccupation. This was growing concern about the obvious decline in Lenin's health, as well as a feeling that insufficient attention was being paid to home security. Stalin, fearing that Lenin's weakening grip on affairs could make opposition forces even more dangerous, exercised his powers as head of the Communist Party Central Committee, to which he had been elected in April 1922. These went as far as to allow him to remove 'unsatisfactory' members of the Politburo, previously considered untouchable. Following Lenin's death, Stalin, in the funeral oration, vowed that he would pick up the flag which had fallen from the hands of 'the genius of the October Revolution'.

By this time, Beria had been promoted to the post of head of the Secret-Political Division of the Transcaucasian OGPU and awarded the Order of the Red Banner, going on to lead the Georgian OGPU. It is not clear when he first met Stalin, but by the late 1920s he was a regular visitor at Stalin's Black Sea summer dacha, and was an obvious source of intelligence about numerous dissident groups in Transcaucasia, the area encompassing Armenia, Azerbaijan and Georgia.

The NKVD emerges

Beria was soon taking a keen interest in the rise of a new instrument of repression destined to replace the OGPU, which had total control of the security apparatus. This was the infinitely more powerful NKVD, which acted as judge, jury and executioner, implementing what were becoming Stalin's ethnic cleansing and genocide programmes. Its tentacles extended deep into the state bureaucracy, and included the GULAG, the acronym for *Glavnor Upravlenie Lagerei* (the Chief Administration of Corrective Labour Camps), the government agency that administered the penal labour camps. A vast network of institutions, populated by men and women who were reduced to the condition of slaves, came under NKVD control. While some of the camps were purely execution centres for political opponents, others, under Beria's growing authority, became a convenient source of emergency labour wherever it was needed, sending out inmates to work on railways, roads, mines and saw mills.

Once the war was underway, some of the camps became arsenals of the Red Army, turning out an endless succession of anti-personnel mines, large-calibre shells and gas masks. Eventually, the NKVD was able to provide 39,000 labourers to produce weapons and ammunition and 40,000 for aviation and tank production.

Additionally, Beria could call on a retinue of able lieutenants, most notably Leonid Zakovsky, who under the OGPU had already prided himself on being the author of a widely-used handbook on torture, giving details of what he considered to be the best methods. These men were soon responsible for carrying out arrests and incarcerations for such transgressions as fraternising with suspect foreigners, or indulging in treasonable talk. Others, masquerading as prisoners and paid in food and extra favours, were insinuated into the camps to report instances of 'slacking' and 'sabotage'. Additionally, NKVD responsibility was assumed for the trials of 'deviationists' and for implementing deportations, resulting in millions being sent either to prison, or to swell the numerous labour battalions. The number of camps grew, in places dominating whole areas, which prompted a memorable description from the writer and dissident Aleksandr Solzhenitsyn, who likened the camps to a chain of islands, 'the Gulag Archipelago'.

As for Beria, as his career advanced, he took scrupulous care to avoid the mistake of others serving the totally unpredictable Stalin. This was the failure to realise that the latter's approval could never be taken for granted. Those who fell out of favour could be removed on a mere whim. Nikita Khrushchev, who himself would eventually become leader of the Soviet Union, declared: 'All of us around Stalin were temporary people.' Stalin's approach to any hint of opposition turned out to be identical both in peace and in war. Disagreement with him on any issue was not only a political matter, but also a capital crime and clear proof of participation in a criminal conspiracy involving nothing less than treason and intent to overthrow the regime.

The killings and atrocities committed by the NKVD were deemed acceptable. In Stalin's eyes, the savage behaviour of Red Army troops could be fully justified. When, during the war, Milovan Djilas, the Yugoslav Communist, complained directly to Stalin that troops were raping Yugoslav women, he received an illuminating lecture on the Russian attitude.

> You have, of course, read Dostoevsky? Do you see what a complicated thing is man's soul, man's psyche? Well then, imagine a man who has fought from Stalingrad to Belgrade – over thousands of kilometres of his own devastated land, across the dead bodies of his comrades and dearest ones? How can such a man react normally? And what is so awful in his having fun with a woman, after such horrors? You have imagined the Red Army to be ideal. And it is not ideal, nor can it be... The important thing is that it fights Germans...'

Throughout his time in Stalin's service, Beria took care to reflect his leader's views, underlining his loyalty to the Bolshevik cause while at the same time being careful to secure his own position, realising how essential it was to his own survival. He went as far as preparing a fulsome oration, which he entitled 'On the History of the Bolshevik Organisations in Transcaucasia', later published as a book for a wider audience, declaring 'Let our enemies know that anyone who attempts to raise a hand against the will of our people, against the will of the party of Lenin and Stalin, will be mercilessly crushed and destroyed.'

Stalin was notorious for engineering the removal not only of political rivals, but also of any source where opposition was likely to occur. Although no firm proof of Stalin's involvement has emerged, one of the most advantageous killings for him happened on 1 December 1934. Forty-eight-year-old Sergei Kirov (born Kostrikov), a former journalist who had risen to be secretary both to the Central Committee and to the Party in Leningrad, as well as gaining membership of the Politburo, was shot in his office by Leonid Nikolaev, a deranged young Party member.

Motives for the killing have preoccupied historians and theorists ever since. Some have claimed that Kirov had refused to give the resentful Nikolaev a job, while others maintained that Kirov's murder was solely the result of jealousy because he had been dallying with Nikolaev's wife. What *is* known is that after firing his revolver Nikolaev attempted to turn the weapon on himself, but he was dragged away, interrogated and subsequently shot.

There was a belief that Stalin had been grooming Kirov, a former favourite, as a possible successor. But it was also known that Kirov, despite his favoured status, had not hesitated on occasions to challenge Stalin on some of his policies. He had argued that those who had suffered after opposing official policy on the creation of collective farms and land to be developed for large-scale agricultural production and industrialisation should be released from imprisonment. When these ideas were raised at the Politburo, a furious Stalin demanded that those who dared to criticise him should be arrested and executed. Furthermore, many of Kirov's disagreements with Stalin had been aired in public, including a call for the readmission of Leon Trotsky, the apostate who had been a leading figure in the Russian October Revolution, second only to Lenin, to the Party.

Kirov and Stalin, as usual that summer, had taken their holiday together, during which Stalin had urged Kirov to reaffirm his loyalty and leave Leningrad for Moscow. Kirov had refused. From then on Stalin saw his protégé as a dangerous loose cannon. Arrests were made of those considered to be Kirov's possible allies, many of whom were 'Old Bolsheviks', yesterday's heroes destined to become today's traitors. They were hustled into police vans and driven to the underground cells of the notorious Lubyanka jail.

These arrests included those of Grigory Zinoviev and Lev Kamenev, left-wing Politburo members seen as 'leading left deviationists' and supporters of Trotsky. The pair had previously fallen out with Lenin over the Bolshevik seizure of power, and had caused Lenin to demand their expulsion from the Party. Stalin accused the Leningrad NKVD of incompetence for not protecting Kirov, and he insisted that those now arrested had been involved with Leonid Nikolaev as part of a larger conspiracy to remove Stalin himself and other leaders. After their trials Zinoviev and Kamenev were sentenced to death and executed.

Whatever the truth, Stalin lost no time in publicly denouncing the 'evil murder of Comrade Kirov, beloved son of the party', and he attended his funeral in Moscow. Outside Russia, it was widely claimed that Stalin had engineered the liquidation. But there were those who discounted any involvement by Stalin, pointing out that he had professional killers at his disposal and would not have employed anyone as mentally unstable as Nikolaev. It was also suggested that if Stalin had wanted to remove Kirov he could have followed established procedures by branding his victim a traitor, arresting him, bringing him to trial and then having him executed by the NKVD as soon as a court had pronounced the sentence.

The Great Purge

Repression and persecution of dissidents, orchestrated by Stalin, became part of what was soon known beyond the Soviet Union as 'the Great Purge'. At the start of the 1930s, purges signified expulsion from the Party, but the meaning was broadened to include imprisonment and even execution, motivated by the desire of Stalin and the Politburo to eliminate all possible sources of opposition. Released Russian archives have put the number of deaths during the Great Purge at 681,692, but other sources cite a figure of two million. This takes into account the arrest of those outside the political category, including 'socially dangerous elements' such as kulaks, a class of landowner who had become independent farmers and supporters of the government of the Tsar, as well as owners of the larger farms and users of hired labour. As such they were designated 'class enemies', who were against the policy of collectivisation.

This was just the beginning. The plenum of the Central Committee of the Communist Party, held in February and March 1937, approved yet more savage methods of dealing with 'enemies of the people', with Leon Trotsky singled out as a figurehead. In his speech Stalin referred to 'Trotskyist wreckers and spies', and the plenum passed a resolution 'instructing the People's Commissariat for Internal Affairs to deal with the unmasking and smashing of Trotskyists and other agents to the very end, in order to crush the least sign of their anti-Soviet activity.' Such activity included past and present support for Trotsky, who was regarded as the arch-traitor.

With the implementation of an order of 30 July 1937, the NKVD, approved by the Bolshevik Party Central Committee, extended its policy of creeping oppression of those deemed by Stalin to be a threat to the security of the state. New categories of those condemned included 'bandits, robbers, thieves, smugglers and swindlers, ex-kulaks, members of anti-Soviet parties, rebels, fascists, spies and the clergy'.

Methods of securing confessions could involve the use of torture, but in many cases ongoing sessions with relays of interrogators at work over hours and days and, in extreme cases, even months or years, produced even better results. Neither food nor sleep were permitted for victims. The temperature in cells was frequently altered and prisoners had bright lights shone in their eyes. Those questioned became automatons with swollen legs and trembling hands, ready to confess to anything. NKVD agents were tempted, on occasions, to carry out arrests, deportations and executions in secret, but court appearances maintained at least the appearance of legality, which, in the early days of the purges, impressed Western observers and Soviet people who knew nothing of NKVD methods.

Beria brought to Moscow

Events in the wake of the assassination of Kirov had been followed closely by Lavrenti Beria, who kept Stalin informed about his own activities in Georgia. By way of recognition, in July 1938 Stalin brought Beria to Moscow as Deputy Head of the NKVD. In charge at the time of his arrival – and thus an obstruction to Beria – was the crippled Nikolai Ivanovich Yezhov, five feet tall and nicknamed 'the Dwarf', the first ethnic Russian to head the NKVD. Only too aware that Beria would set his eyes on his job, and that survival depended on Stalin's whim, Yezhov stepped up his own particular brand of terror, quadrupling the staff at his disposal. These consisted of highly-trained young thugs who were taught that the slightest display of human sympathy was a concession to bourgeois feeling, and above all treachery to the 'class struggle'. Yezhov himself was a notorious sadist, frequently carrying out tortures himself, and having at his disposal equally adept interrogators proficient at beating out confessions.

Executions at the Lubyanka were carried out in the basement. The routine remained standard practice long after Yezhov himself had perished by firing squad. The condemned individual handed in his clothes and was made to change into white undergarments before being taken to the death cell to be shot in the back with a small-bore pistol. Execution with such a weapon frequently necessitated a second shot. If this did not produce the required result, the victim could be struck over the head with a blunt object. A doctor signed the death certificate, while the tarpaulin on the floor was taken away to be cleaned by a woman specially employed for the purpose. Later on, the executions were carried out in an abattoir constructed adjacent to the Lubyanka jail, from where corpses were put into metal boxes and driven to the crematoria.

Yezhov's policy of slaughter of those declared to be actual or perceived traitors was supported by Andrei Vishinsky, a dapper bespectacled lawyer who was to become a notorious figure in a succession of Soviet treason trials. Together with assembled cohorts of the NKVD, the two men preyed on the delegates attending the 17th Party Congress of 1934. Official figures released later indicate that of the 1,966 delegates, 1,108 were eventually shot as enemies of the people. In the same year, one of the most prominent to be arrested was Genrikh Grigoryevich Yagoda, Yezhov's equally ruthless predecessor.

In order to feed Stalin's almost pathological suspicion of existing disloyalties, as well as to ensure their own survival, Yezhov and his NKVD agents focused on the Red Army, hinting that it was preparing to launch a possible *coup d'etat*. The merest suggestion of this was enough for Stalin. No one, regardless of rank, was immune from arrest and Red Army members were subject to the briefest of trials, accompanied by the familiar pattern of sleep deprivation, round-the-clock interrogation and beatings with heavy truncheons.

A notable victim of this hostility was Marshal Mikhail Nikolayevich Tukhachevsky, a former member of the Tsar's Imperial Guard, who went on to become a highly respected chief of the Red Army and a firm advocate of Russian military reform on Western lines. He had made no attempt to conceal his frustration at constant political interference during the Polish–Soviet war in 1920, when he had led the Bolshevik armies against a bid by Poland to extend its borders in the east. He had been forbidden to choose his division commanders or to move his headquarters from Moscow.

This was Tukhachevsky's first clash with Stalin and their disagreements continued into the 1930s. Despite this Tukhachevsky was successful in pressing for military westernisation and radical military reforms, notably the replacement of the traditional reliance on cavalry with a tank-based approach. Red Army officers were invited to German manoeuvres, while officers from the Soviet Union went to Germany on training courses. War games were held between representatives from both countries and were actively encouraged.

NKVD elements close to Stalin represented this modernisation as a joint initiative between Hitler's forces and traitorous elements within the Red Army. Stalin's suspicions hardened. In January 1936 Tukhachevsky visited Britain, France and Nazi Germany. It was claimed subsequently that he had made contact with anti-Stalin exiles and begun plotting against Stalin himself. The allegations reached the ears of General Nikolai Skoblin, a Russian émigré living in Paris, who was a double agent for the NKVD and the Nazi Party's Security Service, the Sicherheitsdienst (SD), which operated with the Gestapo – the Nazi secret state police.

Summoned to the Adlon Hotel in Berlin, Skoblin was questioned by the SD chief Reinhard Heydrich, not only about a possible intended putsch by the Soviet military, but also about Tukhachevsky's attitude towards the Third Reich. Heydrich, and the Schutzstaffel (SS) chief Heinrich Himmler then reported Skoblin's observations to Hitler, who reasoned that if Stalin was warned of an intended putsch it would impel him to move against the army leadership, which would prove an advantage to Germany in the event of war. What was required was documentary proof. Since this was not found, Heydrich's agents, who also included some men from the Abwehr (the German military intelligence), went ahead and concocted it. Documents and letters were prepared, using forgeries of Tukhachevsky's handwriting and signature, and those of other German officers. Two of Yezhov's men travelled to Berlin by a circuitous route, where the Tukhachevsky dossier was handed over in exchange for a payment of three million roubles.

As it turned out, the payment acted as a trap for the Germans and a coup for the NKVD. SS Brigadeführer Walter Schellenberg, head of foreign intelligence, wrote in his memoirs:

> I had personally to destroy most of the three million roubles paid by the Russians, as they consisted of large notes whose numbers had obviously been noted down by the NKVD. Each time that one of our agents tried to use them inside the Soviet Union, he was arrested with record speed.

The execution of Tukhachevsky

On 22 May 1937 Tukhachevsky was arrested and, during a week deprived of sleep, endured battering by the truncheons of the NKVD. At 11.35pm on 11 June he signed a confession with a hand that reportedly streamed blood. He and eight other senior commanders were led off to be shot.

At the same time, Yezhov was becoming increasingly aware that Stalin was intending to replace him. The strain was all too apparent, and there were signs that he was on the edge of alcoholism. He was known to attend executions when drunk, was careless of security and stuffed his unlocked desk with bottles of vodka, and was often too inebriated to attend key meetings. A whispering campaign resulted in Yezhov's arrest five months before the outbreak of war in 1939. In the dead of night he was taken to what had been his own slaughterhouse, with its own soundproof cell, adjacent to the Lubyanka on Dzerzhinsky Street. Here, screaming, he was shot by Vasili Blokhin, the NKVD's chief executioner. Blokhin was well qualified for the job, being a master of what Stalin termed 'black work': assassinations, tortures and intimidation, while officially heading the blandly titled Administrative Executive Department of the NKVD. At the height of his powers his ambitious quota was said to be 300 executions per night.

Beria, who succeeded Yezhov, was installed in new Moscow headquarters with a vast office lit mainly by an electric floor lamp, while air entered through a ventilator. The room had no windows and its walls were hung with thick rugs to deaden all sound. To safeguard his own position and be rid of any of Yezhov's associates who might have proved a threat, Beria gave Stalin a list of those whom he considered should also be removed. Some 340 fell to NKVD firing squads, including some 60 members of the NKVD. According to later accounts, Beria was wise to act swiftly, since Yezhov had previously been marshalling support to bring him down.

Events at home were far from being Stalin's only preoccupation. In Nazi Germany, Hitler, in his increasingly aggressive stance, made no secret of his hatred of the Bolsheviks, coupled with his obsession with *Lebensraum* (living space) in eastern Europe. The Munich agreement of September 1938 had led to the Nazi dismemberment of Czechoslovakia. Stalin, conscious of the dangers of further incursions east and the vulnerability of the Soviet Union, made overtures for an accord with Germany. He received an encouraging response.

Non-aggression pact

During the night of 23/24 August 1939, German Foreign Minister Joachim von Ribbentrop and his Russian counterpart, Molotov, signed a ten-year non-aggression pact in Moscow. Thus much of eastern and northern Europe was divided between Russia and Germany. According to the protocols, the Soviet Union gained a free hand in Finland, Estonia, Latvia, Lithuania and eastern Poland. The subsequent German account of the event reported that, during the ensuing celebrations, Stalin spontaneously proposed a toast to Hitler: 'I know how much the German nation loves its Führer. I should therefore like to drink to his health.'

Meanwhile Beria could be well satisfied with the way his own career was unfolding. He had already been proposed as a candidate for the Politburo, the governing organisation of the Communist Party and of the Soviet state, the highest collegium of the Party elite. *Pravda* carried his inaugural speech, heavy with praise for the 'beloved leader' Stalin, 'the greatest genius of mankind'. Thus, as the Second World war broke out, he found himself in a position of extraordinary power.

Russia's incursion into eastern Poland after the Germans had attacked in the west was driven by Stalin's virulent hatred of the

Poles, which had begun back in 1920 when the Red Army, in its earlier war with Poland, considering itself sure of victory and having pledged to carry the Revolution across Europe to 'water our horses on the Rhine', had been crushed by a devastating Polish attack. Nineteen years later, Stalin was to exact his revenge.

The late Ryszard Kapuscinski, born in Poland and later a writer and journalist, was just seven years old when Soviet troops and the NKVD entered his home town in eastern Poland. He recalled:

> One day a car pulls into the school yard and out step some gentlemen in sky-blue uniforms. Someone says that it's the NKVD. What the NKVD is isn't quite clear, but one thing is certain – when grown-ups utter this name, they lower their voice to a whisper. The NKVD must be terribly important, because its uniforms are elegant, new, spick-and-span...
>
> The NKVD brought us white shirts and red scarves. 'On important holidays', says our teacher in a frightened and sad voice, 'every child will come to school in this shirt and scarf'. They also brought us a box of stamps and distributed them to us. On each stamp was a portrait of a different gentleman. Some had moustaches, others not. One gentleman had a small beard, and two didn't have any hair. Two or three wore glasses. One of the NKVD people went from bench to bench distributing the stamps. 'Children,' said our teacher in a voice that resembled the sound of hollow wood, 'these are your leaders.'
>
> The deportations take place at night. The person is asleep, and suddenly shouts wake him, he sees above him the fierce faces of soldiers and of the NKVD. They pull him out of bed. Shove him with rifle butts, and command him to leave the house. They order that weapons be handed over, which of course no one possesses anyway. The whole time they spew vile obscenities. The worst is when they call someone bourgeois. 'Bourgeois' is a terrible term of abuse. They turn the whole house upside down, and they take the greatest delight in this. During the time they are conducting this whole indescribable mess the wagon arrives.

It is a peasant wagon pulled by a paltry little horse, for the inhabitants of the Polesie region are poor and have bad horses. When the commander sees that the wagon is there he shouts to the ones who will be deported: 'You have 15 minutes to pack and get on the wagon.' If the commander has a kind heart, he gives them half an hour. One simply has to pounce on anything and everything and stuff it into suitcases, whatever one can manage...

The boys who have managed to observe a deportation say that they have followed after these wagons on foot all the way to the railroad tracks. The freight cars stand there, a long transport. Every night there would be a dozen or so wagons, or several score or more...

Those from the escort drove the deportees on, swung their rifles around, shouted, cursed. When they filled one car, they moved on to the next one. What did it mean – to fill a car? It meant to stuff these people into it, using knees and rifle butts so that there would be no room left even for a pin...

Since the time of our house search, Mother does not let us take our clothes off at night. The coats lie on chairs, so they can be put on at the wink of an eye... Mother really does not sleep. She sits at the table and listens the whole time. The silence on our street rings in our ears. If someone's footsteps echo in this silence, Mother grows pale. A man at this hour is an enemy...

One day our teacher disappeared. We arrived at school as usual by 8 o'clock, and after the bell, when we sat down at our benches, the principal, Mr Lubowicki, appeared at the door.

'Children', he said, 'go home now and come back tomorrow, you will have a new teacher, a lady.' Why did they take our teacher? He was constantly nervous and looked out of the window frequently. He would say. 'Ah, children, children', and shake his head. He was always serious and seemed very sad. He was good to us, and if a student stammered while reading Stalin, he didn't shout, and even smiled a little.

I walked home, dejected. As I was crossing the tracks I heard a familiar voice. Someone was calling me. Freight cars stood along the railway, packed with people who were about to be deported. The voice was coming from them. In the door of one of the cars I saw our teacher's face. He was waving to me. My God! I started to race in his direction. But a second later a soldier caught up with me and struck me over the head so hard that I fell. I was getting up, dizzy and with a sharp pain, when he made as if to strike me again but didn't; he only started shouting at me that I should clear out of here, go to the devil.

After the Russians entered eastern Poland oppression was ongoing, with new opportunities for Beria and the NKVD to extend their domain. Hundreds of thousands of citizens of the newly acquired territories were rounded up. Just how many has remained in dispute, but some records have suggested that around 200,000 Poles became prisoners.

One of Beria's first acts was to set up eight camps where captured Polish troops were left to freeze and starve while huddled in pigsties and derelict sheds. Those considered fit to work became forced labourers, building highways in the Carpathian mountains, or were sent to the Ukrainian mines. Prisoners herded into trains were guarded by groups of Soviet militia and menaced by machine guns and rifles. Usually the task of guarding prisoners was in the hands of the regular Red Army regiments, but Beria made sure that these were crack troops from his own NKVD.

Between February 1940 and June the following year, two million Polish mothers and their children were sent to Siberia and central Asia, while their men were destined for concentration camps.

There were no clear motives for individual arrests and many were entirely arbitrary. Lech Kwasiborski's mother Bronislawa, from the village of Gawlike, east of Lwow, had been married for just two days in November 1939 when her husband Emil, an officer in the Polish army, was arrested by the NKVD. She never saw him again. Her son was later to learn what happened to his mother:

The NKVD came for her, reasoning that since her husband was a Polish officer, therefore a spy, so must she be by association. She was herded into a cattle car along with hundreds of Polish doctors, officers, legislators and a cross-section of the Polish intelligentsia. They were transported east, where many were to perish on the frozen steppes of Siberia.

The long and arduous voyage ended in a place called Pawlodarskoja Oblasc, a small town in Asian Kazakhstan. Here they were told how privileged they were to work for the Greatness of the Soviet Republic. One of Bronislawa's tasks was to watch over and protect a fold of sheep, and if any were to vanish she would forfeit her life. One day a few lambs wandered off and mingled with another fold. When she did a count and came up short, despair set in. She went to the other keepers and was fortunate enough to find them. The head shepherd, a Kazakh, however, was shot for losing a lamb.

She had never given up hope of trying to locate her husband, and had made numerous inquiries, always receiving the same reply: 'Write to Papa Stalin and he will reply.' She wrote and never received a reply. She was summoned to the building of the camp council and told her husband was not in Russia and any further questions would not be tolerated...

Amnesty was given to some Poles by the Russians after Germany's 1941 invasion when Stalin, in need of additional forces, allowed the creation of the Polish army on Soviet territory. Bronislawa remained in detention until 1949 and made her way to Canada. Others were not so lucky.

A particularly brutal fate had awaited Pinsk, an agricultural area lying to the south-west of Minsk. Soviet citizenship had been imposed on the entire population, whose inhabitants were issued with compulsory 'internal' passports. Frank Rymaszewski, living in Pinsk, was captured by the NKVD, later recalling that the arrests had begun as soon as the Russian troops arrived. In Grodno, close to the borders of Poland and Lithuania, and at the small town of Chervyenm, near Minsk, NKVD forces carried out the clearance of prisons and mass executions.

First important officials and notables were arrested and executed in the prison yard within days. Soon anybody who wore some kind of a uniform – postmen, railway employees, even boy scouts – was arrested, deemed to be 'ideological enemies'. Those who were not executed were dispersed to the GULAG.

My father, Michal, who was General Manager of the Telephone and Telegraph Office in Pinsk, was already marked by Soviet communist ideology for extermination. All public servants were regarded as 'class enemies' because they 'served the capitalist government'. His arrest followed classic NKVD procedure. Four NKVD men arrived at midnight and took him away. All subsequent enquiries were greeted with the bland assurance that they had never heard of my father, and had no record of his arrest. Eventually they admitted he had been arrested and had been transferred to a prison in Minsk where he was 'awaiting trial'. They refused to accept a food parcel for him and change of underwear. This was the last I ever heard of my father, whom I can only assumed perished in the Soviet Union, like thousands of other unknown Poles: nobody knows where, nobody knows when, nobody knows how.

There was also tangible opposition to the Russian incursion in the Polish–Ukranian city of Lvov, nudging the German–Soviet front line. Reaction to even the mildest dissent was savage. Karol Michal Nawalicki, a 23-year-old law student and dissident from Drohobycz, was arrested in his home town, along with others. That they had been betrayed from within their own ranks seemed certain, particularly as their cache of arms was unearthed and Nawalicki's interrogators had full knowledge of his activities. Almost every session was accompanied by torture. Although resilient to pain, he could not get used to the blows and the beatings. He later wrote:

> During one of these sessions, I noticed a window near me which had none of the usual bars. I concentrated on it to take my mind off the assaults. I was waiting for the right moment to throw myself towards that window, to break the glass and dive head first onto the cobblestones below. I put the plan into action and just managed to break the glass pane... At this very

moment I was grabbed by two members of the NKVD and dragged to my cell.

The prison took in new occupants daily and shuffled others from one jail to another. On the morning of his last day in Drohobycz, to which he was never to return, Nawalicki was transported to the Kolyma camps in the far north-east. Here the political prisoners were intimidated by the presence of rank-and-file criminals, who delighted in terrorising them. Death in the Kolyma camps came in many forms, including overwork, starvation, malnutrition, mining accidents, exposure, murder at the hands of criminals and beatings by the guards. The area, partly within the Arctic Circle, has a subarctic climate where ultra-cold winters last up to six months of the year. After breakfast of soup, bad-smelling herbal tea, two portions of bread, dried fish and five cubes of sugar, the prisoners, tightly packed and standing on open-air platforms, were led to lorries transporting them to the labour camps.

> From our platform we could see very little. Here and there in the deep snow were some dwarfish trees sticking out for miles and miles. Nothing, just endless snow. On the distant horizon was the outline of the mountains, forbidding, cold, like the rest of this panorama of hell. The wind blew with such force that there was a danger of being swept off the platform. Occasionally the sound of the engines almost deafened us and the cold stung right to our bones. I felt that every breath I took froze in front of my face. I was afraid to open my eyes, and end up blind. 'This is the end of the world and of my life', I thought with despair.

Released NKVD files record that the organisation evacuated 750,000 prisoners from 927 camps and 210 labour colonies. Another 140,000 were evacuated from 272 prisons and sent to new ones in the east. Many never made the evacuation and simply vanished. Plans for efficient humane evacuation were non-existent, despite the NKVD's later claims. Passengers in packed trains heading east were either suffocated or blown to pieces by German bombs. In the wake of Barbarossa, a Polish army corporal, Jozef Rodziewicz, was among those hustled from jail by NKVD guards from the small town of

Wilejka, to the east of Vilnius, for a march lasting four and a half days, virtually without rest and totally without food and water, although on Soviet-occupied territory 'the guards' behaviour was bearable'.

> The situation was aggravated by the fact that the German army moved on fast, and one could hear the noise of German planes. The guards used both words and bayonets to make the prisoners walk faster. Soon seven NKVD men were killed by German bombs, while one prisoner was wounded. The second German raid brought similar results. This made the NKVD men mad, especially when they saw the older and weaker people fall down. We all dropped the bundles we had. Those who could not get up by themselves were shot... Instead of shooting, the guards used bayonets to kill those who had fallen. We were hungry but thirst was the worst. Some people bit their lips to get a drop of blood; they also drank their urine.

One Pole, Janusz Puchinski, escaped a burning train with members of his family:

> ...I saw that the train stood in a deep ravine. I thought I would never get out of there. Aeroplanes were screaming over my head, my legs seemed to be made of cotton. Somehow I climbed out, and began running to the woods... When I'd made it, I turned around, and saw that behind me, in the open space, there were crowds of people. At that moment, the next group of planes arrived and began shooting into the crowds...

Aboard the trains, the killings continued. A political prisoner, named as M. Steinberg, evacuated from a prison in Kirovograd, central Ukraine, recorded:

> I dragged behind me my soulmate, Sokolovskaya, for 30 kilometres. She was an old woman, more than 70 years old, completely grey-haired... It was very difficult for her to walk. She clung to me, and kept talking about her 15-year-old grandson, with whom she had lived. The last terror of Sokolovskaya's life was the terror that he would be arrested too. It was difficult for me to drag her, and I began to falter

myself. She told me to 'rest awhile, I'll go alone'. And she immediately fell back by two metres. We were the last in the convoy... I turned back, wanting to get her – and I saw them kill her. They stabbed her with a bayonet in the back. She didn't even see it happen. Clearly they knew how to stab. She didn't even move. Later I realised that hers had been an easy death, easier than that of others. She didn't see that bayonet. She didn't have time to be afraid.

Chapter 2

Murders at Katyn

O n 5 March 1940, Lavrenti Beria, as head of the NKVD, despatched a top-secret memo to Stalin, followed by a sheaf of records of atrocities pre-dating Barbarossa. The overall motive was later revealed to be part of a deliberately calculated strategy to eliminate any likely opposition within Soviet-held areas. The memo's preamble declared:

> A large number of former officers of the Polish Army, employees of the Polish Police and intelligence services, members of Polish nationalist, counter-revolutionary parties, members of exposed counter-revolutionary resistance groups, escapees and others, all of them sworn enemies of Soviet authority, full of hatred for the Soviet system, are currently being held in prisoner-of-war camps of the USSR, NKVD and in prisons in the western provinces of Ukraine and Belorussia.
>
> The military and police officers in the camps are attempting to continue their counter-revolutionary activities and are carrying out anti-Soviet agitation. Each of them is waiting only for his release in order to start actively struggling against Soviet authority.

Beria's memo went on to include as offenders 'former officers of the Polish army and police as well as gendarmes... detained escapees and violators of the state borders' as well as 'hardened and uncompromising enemies of Soviet authority'. Also included were former land and factory owners and government officials. It was recommended by the NKVD that special tribunals should be held to try those detained, but that the defendants should not be informed of the charges or the sentences.

When he singled out the prisoners, Beria was unambiguous about what should follow:

> They are all thorough going enemies of Soviet power, saturated with hatred for the Soviet system... the only reason they want for liberation is to be able to take up the fight against Soviet power. Inmates... should be dealt with by special measures, and the highest measure of punishment, shooting, should be applied to them.

His recommendations were signed by Stalin and agreed by five members of the Politburo. Other moves against the Poles were already ongoing, most notably the movement of two million Polish families to the bleakest areas of Siberia and the harsh daunting landscapes of central Asia. Many, herded into cattle cars, completed their journeys dying of malnutrition and disease. As for those Polish soldiers cited in Beria's memo, there were soon to be some 230,000 in captivity.

On 3 April 1940, the first contingent of Polish officers, numbering around 300, was loaded into buses from a prison camp in the village of Kozelsk near Smolensk. Under NKVD escort and in their uniform they were driven to a small wooded area near the village of Katyn. A diary which was later found on one of the prisoners revealed: 'They took us to a small wood. They took away rings, my watch, belts, knives. What will they do to us?'

There the men were stripped of valuables, belts and knives and led to a large pit dug at the side of the clearing. The last sight the prisoners saw was scores of NKVD men. They were forced to kneel and were shot in the back of the head. The mass graves were cloaked with young birches and fir trees, while dirt tracks, showing the tyre marks of the buses, were covered over. As an attempt at concealment it was only partly successful.

Later, when the Germans invaded eastern Poland, they learnt from local peasants of prisoners being driven into the Katyn forest, of sightings of Russians with picks and spades and above all the sound of gunfire. Other shootings followed, amounting to a total of around 4,500. In addition, Stalin had ordered the further killing of some 22,000 Polish officers and middle-class professional civilians.

Most faced a cruel regime of hard labour, during which many perished, and their fate was to remain unknown. By the following November, it was estimated that one-tenth of the population, largely consisting of priests, officers and aristocrats, had been deported, of whom 31 per cent were dead by 1941, 6,000 arrested and 50,000 shot.

Mass grave

It was not until April 1943 that more information about the events at Katyn emerged. Slave labourers working for the Germans came across a mass grave of officers and soldiers, clad in uniforms that were neither Russian nor German. Scientists from Germany also uncovered seven mass graves of Poles, all of whom had been shot with Russian weapons. Polish and British prisoners of war of the Germans were given access to the remains of Polish army officers massacred at Katyn. Kazimierz Skarzynski, who at the time had been a volunteer with the Polish Red Cross, was called in March 1952 to testify at hearings in Chicago, Illinois, before a select committee investigating the circumstances of the Katyn killings. His testimony to the committee, an extract of which is reproduced here verbatim, revealed:

> The approach to the site was terrible because we saw already 300 bodies exhumed, lying around the grave... killed by a shot through the cranium... We saw some bodies which were tied with a rope. The men had winter clothes. The overcoat was taken off the body and covered the head and then tied with a rope. At the same time the hands were tied backwards with the rope... The coat was put over the body in a way that the slit at the end of the coat was exactly at the place where the revolver had to be applied. I saw one body with the mouth filled with something like sawdust... I have been told by the Germans that there were others. I don't know how many others.

It appeared that Russians at the site had stuffed their victims' mouths before either shooting them or throwing their bodies into a grave. Kazimierz Skarzynski then recalled that a priest from Krakow, who was present, had donned his vestments and called those present to prayer:

He immediately fainted after the prayer... He couldn't stand
the smell. We had to revive him in about half an hour. We
continued to inspect the bodies. After seeing 20 or 50, it is
about the same for 300 or 1,000. They were all in the same
condition.

At around the same time, other priests who had been shot in an
underground prison in Smolensk and their bodies stacked in pits
were buried in Katyn. The Russians continued to blame it all on the
Germans. In 1944, Beria had ordered the setting up of a 'Special
Commission for Ascertaining and Investigating the Circumstances
of the shooting of Polish Officers, Prisoners by the German–Fascist
invaders in the Katyn Forest'. As might have been expected,
members of the commission were handpicked, while NKVD forces
assembled peasants from near the site of the massacre. They were
schooled to say that they had been present when the Germans
brought the prisoners to the forest to be shot.

American diplomats and media representatives had been
summoned to meet the 'witnesses'. Proceedings were held under hot
and blinding klieg lights with whirring cameras. The third secretary
of the American Embassy in Moscow, John F. Melby, was among the
many sceptics, and he later wrote:

During the evening the Commission held a session devoted to
questioning the witnesses... It soon became apparent that the
session was staged for the benefit of the correspondents, and
that the witnesses were merely repeating stories they had
already given the Commission.

Correspondents had only been allowed to question members of the
commission, but not the witnesses, who had been shunted out. The
London-based Polish goverment-in-exile sought another enquiry
through the Red Cross, while Britain, anxious not to offend her
Russian ally, declined to become involved. It took until 1990 before
President Gorbachev finally acknowledged his country's
responsibility for Katyn. Two years later, President Yeltsin gave
Lech Walesa, Poland's leader, evidence of the original order to kill
the officers.

The convoys of death from the Kozelsk prison had not only been conveyed to Katyn. By the middle of May some 4,500 Polish military officers lay buried in eight common graves, the largest containing twelve layers of bodies. Neither were the relatives of the dead immune from the NKVD, whose agents carried out a standard practice. This was to intercept letters that had been sent to the murder victims by their families while in prison. Addresses were traced and their occupants rounded up and deported east.

Kurapaty killing ground

Another infamous killing ground was at Kurapaty, a densely wooded area situated on the outskirts of Minsk, the capital of Belorussia, where allegedly well in excess of 30,000 executions were carried out by invading Germans in 1941. Reliable details were kept firmly under wraps until the impending collapse of the Soviet Union. It was then that Dr Zianon Pazniak, an archaeologist undertaking research into the history of Belorussia and a long-term advocate of its independence, conducted interviews with elderly surviving villagers. They were adamant that no Germans had entered the site and, furthermore, that killings had begun as early as 1937. As a result of his initial findings, Dr Pazniak and a colleague went on to compile further testimonies, in which they cited evidence from 170 witnesses and area residents that informers had been paid to denounce alleged 'enemies of the people' who were then shot and buried in mass graves. To dispose of the evidence at the war's end, all the graves at Kurapaty were dug up and the corpses disposed of.

One witness, Michele Karpovic, related:

> The graves were dug in the first half of the day... In the late afternoon when the trucks started to roll up, the graves had already been dug. The people were shot in batches. They were stood in line and each of them had a gag put in his mouth and tied round with a rag so that he could not spit it out. The executioners wore NKVD uniforms...
>
> When they had shot one batch, they threw a bit of earth on top of the heap of bodies, smoothed it over, so that it was all level, and brought up the next batch.

According to another witness, the presence of the lorries containing the bodies of those who had been shot became a routine sight, present seven days a week, often throughout the night. 'When they started shooting, you could hear moaning, weeping, cursing.'

Here, once again, Vasili Blokhin was the chief protagonist. He also journeyed to a camp which was carrying out the killings of captured Poles at the town of Ostashkov, north-west of Moscow. Here the prisoners were led to a soundproofed chamber and shot in the back of the neck. Dressed in a leather apron, helmet and gauntlets, Blokhin supervised the killings. A model bureaucrat, he telegraphed a body count to Moscow each evening. Between twenty and thirty local NKVD agents, guards and drivers were pressed into service to escort prisoners to the basement, confirm their identification, then remove the bodies and hose down the blood after each execution. The executions were conducted at night, starting at dark and continuing until just prior to dawn.

The first week of Barbarossa saw the Russians verging on panic as the Wehrmacht divisions swept all before them. NKVD agents either hastily evacuated prisoners from jails or indulged in mass slaughter. In the wake of the evacuations, it became a matter of routine for members of families left behind to rush to the jails in the faint hope of finding anyone who might have escaped the round-ups. In many cases they found corpses so badly mutilated by torture that positive identification proved impossible.

For the NKVD there was a killing spree in the western Ukraine. In Sambit, they dynamited cells that were either crammed with women or stacked to the ceiling with rotting, decomposing corpses, smelling so vile that no one had the stomach to remove them. Either that or bodies had been chopped up, their tongues, ears, eyes and matted hair strewn around the floors.

All the while, the Russian authorities continued to raise still more reserves within the NKVD to serve in the front line in the face of the seemingly inexorable German advance. Stavka, the Soviet High Command, went on to issue the order:

Concerning the formation of Rifle and Motorised divisions of the NKVD troops personnel 00100 29 June 1941. Immediately proceed to the formation of 15 divisions... For the formation of these divisions a proportion of NKVD border guards and internal security personnel should be employed, including privates, NCOs and commissioned officers.

The People's Commissar of Internal Affairs L.P. Beria should be charged with the responsibility of raising these Divisions; Red Army's Chief of Staff should provide the divisions being raised with the necessary personnel, material resources and weapons...

Stavka of High Command
Timoshenko
Stalin
Zhukov

The divisions were badly needed, as was a ruthless tightening of discipline. All too soon it was the turn of the city of Lvov, in western Ukraine, to fall to the Germans in a nightmare of carnage and chaos. In total panic following the withdrawal of the Red Army, the NKVD carried out mass shootings in the jails, only to face a Ukrainian-led uprising which engulfed the city. Consequently the NKVD was obliged to abandon the jails; inmates at the central prison of Brygidka seized the opportunity to force their way out. Others, fearing retaliation from any remaining guards, remained where they were; a grim mistake, as it turned out, since sections of the NKVD returned to machine-gun them. Amid the chaos, there were fortunate survivors but, in a final outburst of violence, the Red Army murdered some 10,000 inmates from a number of other jails.

Stalin's overall aim was to achieve a compact area of defence for the USSR as well as recovering territory previously held by the tsars. As had been set out in the protocols to the German-Soviet non-aggression pact, which gave Russia the right to station troops in the Baltic states, he demanded that Estonia, Latvia and Lithuania remain within the Soviet sphere. Predictably, the strong NKVD presence in these areas was orchestrated by Beria. As Commissar of International Affairs, he lost no time in pleading with Stalin for increased troops and equipment for his special forces within the NKVD.

At a meeting with generals at the Kremlin, many of Beria's pleas were greeted with considerable misgivings by the orthodox military, whose members felt that, if he had his way, power would shift irrevocably to the NKVD. His plans included securing the total loyalty of Ivan Aleksandrovich Serov, who joined the NKVD at the outbreak of the war, becoming his Deputy Commissar of State Security. A man of considerable brutality, Serov had figured in many secret police actions, including the deportations of Caucasians and groups within the Baltic states.

Merciless deportations

Serov's instructions to those carrying out deportations were as merciless as they were precise. The knock on the door of homes that were housing deportees was to be in the middle of the night. Entry was to be made by two NKVD NCOs, accompanied by a couple of soldiers and a civilian member of the militia wearing a red armband. All the deportees were to be searched, along with the premises, in order to discover any hidden arms. An official directive instructed:

> ...The senior member of the operative group shall assemble the entire family of the deportee in one room... In view of the fact that a large number of deportees must be arrested and distributed in special camps and that their families must proceed to special settlements in the region, it is essential that the operations of removal of both the members of the deportee's family and its head shall be carried out simultaneously, without notifying them of the separation confronting them.

A victim of Serov's campaign recalled what happened to a family in eastern Poland at four o'clock in the morning on 10 February 1940:

> When they banged on the door I was the first to open it and I was facing a soldier with a fixed bayonet poking into my chest. The NKVD man asked if I was so-and-so. I said 'Well, I'm the son, my mother is the owner of this property'. So they told me to open the door and once inside the NKVD man took a document from his briefcase. I can still remember my

amazement when I saw that a major document which related to our deportation was written on a cement bag. Just brown paper from a cement bag. He read the document which accused us of being hostile to the peace-loving Soviet Union and said that we were going to be deported for re-education.

We were not expecting anything like this. Up to this time there had been no deportations. OK, some people had started to talk – why were the trains of cattle trucks waiting at the local railway station? But the train had been there for some time and people stopped being bothered about it...

We took all the food we could carry. But all the farm and livestock equipment we had to leave behind, of course. Before I left, the last job I did was to let the guard dog off the chain and to take some hay for the animals. They took us to the station on a sledge.

When they reached the station, the deportees found themselves in the company of hundreds of others. They were locked in their wagons for as long as three weeks, throughout their journey to the GULAG, enduring the stench of unwashed bodies and clothes and primitive latrines.

Moves against other countries included Estonia, which from September 1939 had been forced to accept Russian bases on her soil. Troops of the Red Army carried out the military occupation, while Beria's men made mass arrests of entire families living in the area. Hundreds of cattle cars, choked with prisoners, made their way to the Ural mountains and to villages abutting the Chinese border.

Moves against Latvia were already in progress. An earlier threat had been delivered with typical bluntness by Stalin during a meeting with Vilhelms Munters, the Latvian foreign minister: 'I tell you frankly, a division of spheres of interest has already taken place. As far as Germany is concerned, we could occupy you.' To underline Stalin's point, Soviet warships were present, as were two tank corps, two cavalry divisions and six infantry divisions, which were holding manoeuvres on the Latvian border. By the end of August 1940, a Soviet Latvian Constitution had been promulgated, giving birth to the Latvian People's Commissariat of State Security, ensuring power for NKVD commissars. Directions on procedures were signed on 28 November 1940 in the city of Kaunus by the Lithuanian NKVD commissar, and were in line with those issued by Moscow to their Latvian and Estonian counterparts. The circular order read in part:

> ...*November 28, 1940*
>
> For the task of operative work, it is of profound importance to know how many former policemen, White Guardists, ex-army officers, members of anti-Soviet political parties and organisations are in the territory of Lithuania and where this element is concentrated. This is necessary in order to define the counter-revolutionary force and to direct our apparatus of active agencies for their annihilation and liquidation.
>
> Executing the Order of the People's Commissar of NKVD of USSR, No.001223, referring to a report on the anti-Soviet element, and the demand to be most careful in the exact execution of that task, I issue the following order:
>
> Into the alphabetic files must be entered all those persons who, because of their social and political past, their nationalistic-chauvinistic inclinations, religious beliefs, moral and political instability, are hostile to the socialistic form of State, and consequently might be exploited by foreign intelligence services and counter-revolutionary centres for their anti-Soviet purpose.
>
> Among such elements are to be counted:
>
> a) All former members of anti-Soviet political parties, organisations and groups: Trotskyites, right-wingers, Mensheviks, Social Democrats, anarchists etc.
> b) All former members of nationalistic, chauvinistic, anti-Soviet parties, Nationalists, Christian Democrats, the active members of student fraternities, of the National Guard etc.
> c) former policemen, officers of the criminal and political police and of prisons...

Puppet government

The establishment of a puppet government was followed by the announcement that there would be parliamentary elections to ensure a 'free and independent' Latvia. As it turned out, voters had to choose from a list of Party-approved candidates sanctioned by Andrei Vishinsky, Deputy Commissioner of Foreign Affairs, who had served as Stalin's legal aide during the Communist Party purges. A stumbling block for the authorities was the likelihood that many people would refrain from voting in protest. It was thus required that official identity documents would have to be produced when voting, and these would be stamped. Those who were found to be without a stamp were designated 'enemies of the people'. Workers from factories and offices were marched in groups to the polling centres. The Soviet News Agency announced subsequently that 94.8 per cent of those eligible voted and that 97.8 per cent of the voters cast their ballots in favour of the approved candidates. The 'elected' puppet parliament assembled on 21 July 1940. The earlier intention to create a 'free and independent' Latvia was conveniently forgotten; it was absorbed by the Soviet Union on 5 August, a fate soon shared by Lithuania and Estonia.

The premises of the abolished Ministries of Home and Social Affairs, situated in the centre of Riga, were commandeered as the main NKVD headquarters. On any pretext, those who were considered 'unreliable' were called in for interrogation. The ground floor and cellars were remodelled into special interrogation prisons and equipped with cells so small that they were nicknamed 'dog kennels'. Prisoners were given the choice of standing or lying down. Interrogation rooms had instruments to break the bones of arms and shins, to pierce feet, to squash noses and testicles and to pull nails and skin. Prolonged beatings of uncooperative prisoners became commonplace. After each session, victims were put into the cells to 'recover', a prelude for further interrogations, usually beginning late in the evening and going on throughout the night, with the purpose of extorting confessions. No one, including the militia, Workers Guard, Bolshevik party members, candidates for office, members of the Communist youth and assorted organisations, was exempt from NKVD orders. The Latvian army, seen as a possible centre of resistance, was transformed into the 24th Rifle Corps of the Red Army, also designated the Territorial Rifle Corps, its manpower released (in fact, effectively dismissed) from active duty and replaced by 'reliable' Russians. Arrests became routine, heralded by the dread knock on the door in the small hours.

Following Stalin's death in 1953, some individual accounts of family tragedies emerged, among them that of Lt Col. Karlis Zalitis of the Latvian army, who succeeded in shooting the NKVD officer sent to arrest him. Determined that his wife and daughter would not be captured, he attempted to kill them, then turned the gun on himself. Unconscious, he was swiftly transported to NKVD headquarters, where he died. Although his wife survived, his daughter, slightly wounded, was deported to Siberia.

Elsewhere the Russians by no means always had their own way. One of Stalin's long-standing grudges had been against his tiny neighbour, Finland, which until 1917 had been part of the Russian Empire. Following the creation of the treaties giving the Soviet Union the right to station troops in Baltic bases, similar pressure was put on Finland, one of the chief motives being to secure improved defences for the vital city of Leningrad.

To achieve this Stalin made two demands: a naval and air base at the mouth of the Baltic at Hanko, on Finland's southernmost tip, and the cession of the Keratin isthmus, situated between the Gulf of Finland and Lake Ladoga, north of Leningrad. The Finns stoutly refused and negotiations were broken off, in the prelude to what became known as the Winter War.

In hope of an easy victory, the Red Army advanced on Finland on 30 November 1939, its progress slow amidst frozen lakes and within deep, tree-lined gullies. More than a million men encountered swift resistance at heavy cost. More than 200,000 were killed, many harassed by white-clad ski patrols. Standard military equipment had limited effectiveness in the snow-covered forests. The Russians had been forced to fight on a small front, despite the sheer size of the Russian-Finnish border, much of which was impassable. The Finns benefited from being able to get a fair idea of the route any Russian advance would be obliged to take. Their platoons, thoroughly at home in the northern polar nights, had advanced in disciplined silence, stabbing their enemy with the long knives that were their standard equipment. Thousands of Russians were evacuated through injury, burns, disease and the effects of frostbite. Food supplies took days to reach the front lines. Russian tanks, often crewed by inexperienced drivers and mechanics, broke down in temperatures of minus 30 degrees centigrade.

NKVD troops, who were well armed for the purpose, were assembled behind the lines specifically to shoot deserters and stragglers, as well as units seeking to leave the battlefield. Border guards and firing squads at the front were ready to execute officers accused of cowardice and incompetence at on- the-spot tribunals. The Finnish victory, however, was reversed in February 1940 when the Russians, somewhat fortified, regained the initiative. The Red Army eventually broke through in the south. Marshal Semyon Timoshenko commanded forces in the region of Karelia, ordering saturation bombing of a line of earthworks defending Finland's border. The barrage lasted two weeks, after which the Russians advanced, meeting small resistance. On 12 March 1940, the Finns surrendered.

'Never retreats'

During the months leading up to Barbarossa, Beria had been intent on gaining a high profile, forever pleading with Stalin for units of elite troops to be transferred from the Red Army to his own special forces, and having them equipped with the best weaponry available. This created widespread resentment within the Red Army, many of whose officers maintained that the NKVD had sufficient resources, but Stalin acceded to Beria's demands. His troops were termed Select Special Forces and given their own slogan: 'The Soviet Soldier Never Retreats'.

The price for Russia of engaging with Finland was appalling. For some 5,000 who had been taken prisoner by the Finns and subsequently released, the fate was grim. Article 58 of the Soviet Criminal Code forbade Soviet soldiers, even the wounded, to surrender. Indeed, the Soviet government viewed being taken prisoner as desertion and treason. Many of the troops were deported and were never heard of again.

To repair the damage to Stalin's reputation, which could scarcely be concealed from the Allies, Timoshenko was appointed to undertake vital military reforms. Party commissars, dedicated to political supervision of the armed forces, were swept aside, the emphasis shifting to military professionals. Back into favour came the traditional officer corps, previously scorned as outdated. More than 1,000 men were promoted to admiral or general, while those uniforms, which had earlier been abolished, were reinstated.

On the other hand, the role played by Beria's border guards and firing squads in removing deserters won Stalin's approval and the 'For Valour' medal. As Chief of the Secret Police and People's Commissar of Internal Affairs, Beria's authority within the NKVD appeared absolute. Increasingly, NKVD activities within diplomatic circles spread way beyond the Soviet Union. Every Russian embassy, consulate or mission had an NKVD resident in charge with powers over all staff, consuls and ambassadors included. Regular reports were also received from Communist parties in Europe and North America. Soviet radio, press and literature survived censorship only if they avoided any criticism of official policy. Those who refused to admit to offences ran the risk of arrest along with the members of their family, including young children.

No one, however competent, was immune from Beria. One of the leading figures who had achieved conspicuous success against the Finns was General Kirill Meretskov, given the rank of Hero of the Soviet Union and afterwards made Chief of the General Staff and then Deputy Commissar of Defence. He was sent, in the wake of Barbarossa, to the North-Western Front headquarters to act as Stavka representative. But his political antennae were weak, and he failed to avoid a clash with the eternally jealous Beria, who in a fit of envy accused him of being a traitor and had him thrown into jail for the mandatory torture. The act incurred the fury of Stalin, who at the time was badly in need of competent generals. After his release, according to witnesses, Meretskov was received sympathetically by Stalin, who blandly enquired 'How are you feeling?'

Focus on Poland

Russian attention focused on Poland. In the thick of the German invasion, Lieutenant General Wladyslaw Anders, in charge of two divisions of Polish infantry and a cavalry brigade, was squeezed with his men between the advancing Germans and the Russian armies coming in from the east. Soon he was lying in a forest half-dead from eight wounds, his divisions broken and scattered. Taken under Soviet guard to a Polish hospital, he was told plainly that he could only hope to save his life by enlisting in the Red Army. His loyalty to his country was already a byword and he refused. It was all the Russians needed. He was held first at Lvov, where:

> ...more than a dozen NKVD men suddenly rushed into my room and forcibly dragged me from my bed and out of the ward... My slow movement down the stairs on my crutches irritated them, and they gave me a push so that I fell down. This was repeated on each flight of stairs.
>
> I was... shoved into a small room with a half-wrecked stove and a barred window without panes... The temperature [was] below freezing... Occasionally a bit of bread was thrown in. Every [few]... days, NKVD men would burst in at night and carry out a most careful examination of the cell, [including] the long beard which had grown during my imprisonment and which was stiff from pus that had run into it from my frost-bitten face. I was kicked and beaten on these occasions.

Again he was given the option of joining the Red Army or confessing to crimes he had never committed. When he refused, he was transferred to the NKVD's Lubyanka jail in Moscow.

In the Lubyanka

The recollections of those who served their sentences in the Lubyanka and who survived broadly agree in their accounts of life in a complex of three buildings. The main building contained the prison that predated the Russian Revolution of 1917. The regime consisted of strict rules from which there was no deviation, one of the most exacting of which was a ban on ordinary speech – only whispering was permitted at any time. A rigid schedule was enforced for just about every activity, including going to the lavatory and the serving of meals. Observation was unremitting; guards stared through small apertures in the prison door every few minutes. Cells were required to be spotless and had to be cleaned and polished daily by the occupants.

Newly arrived prisoners did well to seek advice from those who had been serving sentences of some length. They learnt that it was common practice for interrogators to menace their victims by piling their desks with loads of papers and documents, which looked as if they provided incriminating evidence of their victim's guilt, but which in fact had no relevance at all.

During his time in the Lubyanka, Anders gained further insight into the awesomely efficient investigative methods of the NKVD. In a bid to impress him, the minutest details of his service career were recalled with accuracy, along with intimate snapshots of himself which he had never known existed.

Anders's eventual release, which came after a stay which had been largely spent in solitary confinement, was a surprise. He was ushered into the presence of Beria, who informed him that Germany had attacked Russia and that he had been 'elected' commander-in-chief of the new Polish army to be organised inside the Soviet Union. Overnight, Anders, with no relief from his multiple wounds in back and hip, had been saved from the attentions of the NKVD and transformed from being an 'enemy of the people' into a Soviet ally. The reality was that Barbarossa had forced Stalin to make some recognition of the Polish government-in-exile.

Another victim in the hands of the NKVD was Szymon Zaremba, a teenager from a land-owning family in Pyrzowice, western Poland, who had made a journey east to join the army. It was his misfortune to fall into the hands of the NKVD and be force-marched for two days as far as Zytomierz in the Ukraine.

NKVD interrogators were firmly under political direction from Moscow and received detailed instructions. Certainly, they beat up and tortured prisoners but did so for a declared purpose rather than to inflict pain and suffering for the sake of it, which was the case with many Gestapo interrogators. Since the early days of the purges they had learnt that to deprive a prisoner of, say, three days sleep could provide excellent results with less effort. In the circumstances, I was fortunate. My interrogators reasoned that since I was just a youth and not a member of any dissident Polish group, strong arm methods would have produced nothing for the simple reason that I knew nothing. I had merely been in search of adventure in the army so they contented themselves by haranguing and threatening me.

Eventually they lost interest and housed me and a few others in a nearby building. We lost little time in looking around for possible ways to escape. There were stables next door and we volunteered to look after the horses there. As casually as we could, I and another prisoner hitched a couple to a cart and drove slowly to the gates. We were challenged by a guard who demanded to know where the hell we thought we were going. I explained – blatant spur-of-the-moment lie, of course – that we had got permission to get some hay to feed the horses. At that moment a car load of Russian officers drove up. To their aggressive questioning, I pleaded that one of the horses had gone lame and the rest needed food. They showed no interest, merely shrugged and let us go.

Ahead of them lay a long and perilous return to western Poland, where Zaremba undertook dangerous work raising bands of partisans, with whom he threw in his lot.

Liquidation of Trotsky

Meanwhile, on their home ground, the Russians had much unfinished business, some of which was the concern of Lavrenti Beria. One pressing concern was the liquidation of Stalin's one-time rival, Leon Trotsky, in exile in Mexico and already under sentence of death *in absentia*. Trotsky was known to be writing his political memoirs, which would certainly contain material that could damage Stalin's image as the benevolent father of the Soviet Union, and expose him as the tyrant responsible for the excesses of the Great Purge. Revelations of this kind would undermine previous bland accounts, including some prepared or written by Beria himself.

On his arrival in Mexico, Trotsky had settled into a large dilapidated house in the town of Coyoacan and employed loyal bodyguards. The local Communist Party, acting on instructions from

Moscow, released plenty of allegations that he was plotting against the Mexican government and 'collaborating with fascist and reactionary elements'.

Both Trotsky and his wife, Natalia, felt the noose tightening. Their guards watched, suspicious of the number of strangers and vehicles driving perpetually around the house. All visitors were screened and Trotsky was under no illusions that the NKVD knew too much about him to let him survive and had asked the local authorities for increased protection.

The first attempt on his life came on 24 May 1940. Beria set up an elaborate death squad, whose members were kitted out with bogus police and army uniforms. They carried a full armoury of sub-machine guns, home-made incendiaries and dynamite bombs. Equipped with ladders, grappling hooks and a power saw, they forced their way into the apartment, raking it with fire and setting off the incendiaries. Trotsky and Natalia survived by lying under a bed. Their grandson Seva was slightly injured and two sentries were overpowered. The raiders then departed, leaving a time-bomb behind them which failed to go off. The sole victim was a security guard, who had been tricked into admitting the gang. He was dragged away, murdered and his corpse tossed into a lime pit.

For the second attempt, Belorussian-born Naum Eitingon, a seasoned NKVD agent previously based in Spain, recruited a young Spaniard and fanatical Stalinist, Ramon Mercador, whose mother had worked for the NKVD as a Russian spy during the Spanish Civil War. Mercador gained Trotsky's confidence, joining him in his study over many evenings. On this particular day, 21 August 1940, Trotsky was reading an article written by Mercador, who was standing behind him. In a swift movement the younger man took from his jacket a specially sharpened Alpine ice-axe. With it he struck Trotsky with some force, but the blow was not sufficient to kill his victim. In his agony, Trotsky shouted to his guards, who hurried into the study: 'Don't kill him', Trotsky told them. 'He has a story to tell'. Rushed to hospital and on his death bed, he was reported as having said in English: 'I feel here... that this is the end... This time they've succeeded'. Mercador, himself in hospital after receiving a severe beating from Trotsky's guards, readily confessed to the killing, posing for photographs and demonstrating how he had used the ice-axe. He was sentenced to 20 years for the murder. His connection with the NKVD was not revealed until after the fall of the Soviet Union.

Internal reform

After Trotsky's removal, Stalin considered that it was time to call a halt to further purges. His emphasis switched to substantial reform of the internal security machine. A law of 3 February 1941 took the Chief Office of State Security out of the hands of the NKVD, turning that office into an independent ministry or People's Commissariat, the NKGB (*Narodnyi Komissariat Gozudarstvennoi Bezopastnosti*). Its remit included organising counter-espionage throughout the USSR, liquidating anti-Soviet parties and counter-revolutionary formations and guarding senior figures. In charge was Vsevolod Nikolayevich Merkulov, a former associate of Beria, who had served as his deputy in the Caucasus.

Stalin, meanwhile, was working on a broader front, contemplating further appeasement of Germany, believing that Hitler would not contemplate invading Russia since this would result in him fighting a war on two fronts. To nourish Stalin's belief, the German Abwehr was quick to spread rumours that Hitler was preparing to issue an ultimatum, demanding fresh concessions from the Soviet Union rather than preparing for war. Beria, only too aware of the danger of opposing Stalin on any issue, was in a serious dilemma. He was careful to express his indignation at those within the NKVD who dared to send reports of alleged preparations for a German invasion. Such men, he declared: 'should be ground into labour camp dust'. With oozing sycophancy, he wrote to his leader on 21 June 1941, declaring:

> I again insist on recalling and punishing our ambassador to Berlin, Dekanozov, who keeps bombarding me with 'reports' on Hitler's alleged preparations to attack the USSR. He has reported that this attack will start tomorrow... But I and my people, Iosif Vissarionovich, have firmly embedded in our memory your wise conclusion: Hitler is not going to attack us in 1941!

At the same time, there was no way that Beria could avoid relaying the findings of his NKVD border guards, who reported that German saboteurs had infiltrated the Ukraine, Belorussia and Lithuania, carrying radio transmitters, weapons, currency and Russian passports. A telephone cable had been found at the bottom of the San River, in south-east Poland, which had been used to monitor the telephone conversations of the Red Army. Additionally, there were numerous instances of German aircraft violating Soviet air space. Further signs of German intentions were forwarded to Moscow by Dekanozov, who reported that he had been seeking a meeting with Hitler in vain, in order to complain about 180 intrusions into Soviet air space. A note to von Ribbentrop, who had conveniently absented himself from Berlin, was ignored.

Following the launch of Barbarossa, Beria had been quick to assure Stalin that he was in full control of a highly effective security apparatus. To this end, the earlier arrangement was reversed and state security was again placed under the NKVD. Stalin appointed Beria General Commissar of State Security. In addition to the vastness of the GULAG, Beria was in absolute control of the regular prisons, the police force, fire protection and border, internal, railroad and convoy troops. To this end, Beria instituted a clean sweep of top NKVD posts, in addition becoming deputy chairman of the USSR Council of Ministers, which was the highest state body. It now remained to be seen how the strengthened security apparatus would conduct itself within a fresh climate of total war.

Chapter 3

Tightened Repression

Germany's plan for Barbarossa had been set out on 18 December 1940 as Directive No.21. Signed by Hitler, it stated: 'The German Armed Forces must be prepared, even before the conclusion of the war against England, to crush Soviet Russia in a rapid campaign. The bulk of the Russian army, stationed in western Russia, will be destroyed by daring operations led by deeply penetrated armoured spearheads.'

The likelihood of the Germans launching a surprise attack had earlier been suggested to Stalin by Zhukov, but the Soviet leader had brushed him aside. Warnings, however, did not go away, which was a source of particular frustration to the NKVD, who had a highly-placed agent within the German community in Tokyo. This was Richard Sorge, a loyal Communist who, under cover as a roving journalist, had been despatched first to various European countries with orders to test the strength of Communist feeling. He then went on to Tokyo, where he established an espionage ring, gaining extra cover editing the German embassy news bulletin, which enabled him to study official press releases from Berlin.

In May, Sorge sent Moscow further warnings of Hitler's intentions, including a claim that a German attack would begin that month with no ultimatum or declaration of war. In an outburst of fury, Stalin declared that Sorge 'was a little shit who has just set himself up with some good business in Japan'. Even anti-Nazi sources in Moscow who issued further warnings were disregarded, with Hitler's intentions declared to be bluff.

When Barbarossa finally got underway, Germany's star seemed in the ascendant. The fortunes of Hitler and his Wehrmacht appeared encouraging. Three primary targets had been envisaged: Leningrad, Moscow and Kiev. Field Marshal Fedor von Bock's Army Group Centre appeared to be well on the way to Moscow, while Panzer Group 3 under General Hermann Hoth, together with General Heinz Guderian's Panzer Group 2, had surged through waving grassland and wheat fields towards Minsk to the east of the German-Soviet border through occupied Poland.

Throughout the advance, the Jews were to be the object of systematic and brutal destruction. On 22 June, Wehrmacht forces stormed into the city of Lutsk in north-west Ukraine where, as was soon to become apparent, both sides were guilty of atrocities. In the city's hospital, the Germans found a Jewish doctor operating on a Christian patient. When ordered to stop, he resolutely refused and was dragged to his home and slaughtered with his entire family.

During their retreat from Lutsk, the NKVD, many of them in panic, forced most of the city's Jewish inhabitants to make for a ghetto. They were lined up outside and machine-gunned by Soviet tanks with the subsequent justification that they had intended to escape. Those who managed to survive the onslaught were ordered to stand up and bury the dead. They too were then mown down.

Red Army disaster

Not everything went well for the Germans. As the war progressed, the presence of a breakaway faction, the Ukrainian Insurgent Army, dedicated to the formation of a independent Ukrainian state, created a resistance group and guerilla army which was to secure support within Germany, Poland and the Soviet Union. However, the Red Army also had its share of disaster. The commander of the Western Front (army group), General Dmitri Pavlov, striving to escape a pincer movement had, against orders, pulled back his reserves, only to be overtaken on both flanks by the rapid advance of Hoth and Guderian. It was a miscalculation which left Minsk virtually undefended. Another loss was the old border fortress of Brest-Litovsk, lying to the west, all but annihilated with the surrender of 7,000 Russians. The Russians, however, did manage to maintain some resistance in the area, despite fierce German bombing. Their defence included forces of the 17th NKVD Border Guards

Detachments and the 132nd Independent NKVD Battalion, a total of around 3,500 men. By 9 July, when Minsk finally fell, some 324,000 prisoners had passed into captivity, along with the loss of 3,300 tanks and 1,800 field guns. The Germans, despite the tough Soviet resistance, flooded into the city.

As for General Pavlov, his career lay in ruins, in sharp contrast to his status from the mid-1930s onwards, when he had seen service on the Republican side during the Spanish Civil War, commanding a tank brigade. He had become a Hero of the Soviet Union, then Head of the Directorate of Tank and Armoured Car Troops, rising to be General of the Army. After the Minsk debacle, determined to fight, he established new headquarters in Mogilev, well to the east. It was to prove a brief, uneasy breather.

Meanwhile, Beria's responsibilities in Moscow as head of the NKVD remained formidable, but to his chagrin his powers had to be shared. He was increasingly obliged to work with the Political Administration of the Red Army (PURKKA), headed by a Jew from Odessa, Lev Zakarovich Mekhlis, who had been an office boy and schoolteacher, executive director of *Pravda* newspaper and a member of the Red Army's Supreme Military Council. Mekhlis, adept at intrigue, had served as a ruthless commissar in the Crimea during the Russian Civil War, having first met 'my dear Comrade Stalin' during the Polish campaign. Mekhlis controlled the *politruk*, government-appointed officers whose duty was to oversee military units, further defined as 'education work'. This meant a ruthless programme of surveillance which no one, least of all the command staffs of the various armies and fronts, could avoid. The officers reported constantly on matters of morale and discipline, instances of desertion, drunkenness, insubordination and absence without leave. As a result of Stalin's deep-seated suspicion of the Red Army came a demand that all officers and men escaping from the German encirclement be rigorously investigated. The result was tightened repression intended to keep troops firmly in the battle line.

To achieve this, security units were redesignated Special Sections (*OOs – Osobye otdely*), ultimately responsible to the NKVD. Their orders were to prevent soldiers leaving their battle positions; to check and if necessary arrest officers and men suspected of abandoning their posts; to execute deserters on the spot; and to carry out the sentences of courts martial, if necessary by executing in front of their comrades those found guilty.

Mekhlis, a bully whose cruelty was legendary, went on to secure the post of Political Commissar of the Red Army, which gave him power as Stalin's supreme and tireless troubleshooter to issue death sentences to all troops, regardless of rank or circumstances. Any officer showing scruples or reluctance to mow down women and children in the path of the advance was likely to be shot.

In early August 1941, the 28th Army was encircled and totally destroyed at a village near Smolensk, following its heavy counter-attack from the south in an attempt to relieve other forces. The commander, Lieutenant General Vasili Kachalov, was killed in heavy combat, along with a small group of soldiers who had succeeded in breaking out of the main encirclement, only to be caught by German forces on the way to the safety of the Soviet lines. Because Kachalov's death could not be confirmed, he was listed at first as missing in action. Then came the announcement from Stavka on 16 August, which charged that Kachalov 'while locked in encirclement, together with his staff group, displayed cowardice and surrendered to the German fascists.' The NKVD stepped in; the general's wife and mother-in-law went to the GULAG.

As subsequent post-war investigations were to show, the charge was totally false, based on Stalin's malevolent desire to transfer guilt for the Smolensk defeat to Kachalov and his subordinate military commanders. No record of surrender was found. The next grotesque development was sentencing Kachalov *in absentia* to 'the highest degree of punishment, execution by firing squad and deprivation of military rank'. It was not until 13 February 1954 that the well-supported testimony of others who had been abroad revealed the truth: Kachalov had been killed in his tank during the fighting.

Blocking Detachments

Instances of consummate ruthlessness were provided by the blocking detachments of the special sections which came into being in June 1941. These were the creation of the 3rd Department of

Russia's Ministry of Defence, responsible for seizing those who had roused their suspicions, notably troops seen to be retreating. Placed in the immediate rear of wavering divisions, they were required, in the event of panic and disorderly withdrawals, 'to execute on the spot cowards and those spreading panic, so assisting the division's loyal soldiers to discharge their duty to the Motherland'. At first, the detachments were under Red Army control, but steadily became the responsibility of the NKVD, which maintained its own large military force of internal security and border troops, organised into fifteen infantry divisions with their own tanks and artillery.

Right from the onset of war, the border troops were a reserve force for the regular military units. No time was lost: the NKVD formed them into infantry divisions. In the face of the German advance, the main function of both border and internal forces was to secure the Red Army's rear. As time went on, their responsibilities increased.

Early on, Beria made it clear that in no way did his NKVD regard itself as part of the regular army. Although men wore standard army uniform, they sported distinctive badges and headdress to highlight what they regarded as their exclusivity. Border guards wore green and blue caps and green shoulder straps, whereas internal troops had red and blue caps and red shoulder straps. An exception were members of the secret police, a group apart with their distinctive army insignia with no embellishments that would have identified them as part of the NKVD, an advantage when it came to assignments where their identity had to be kept under wraps.

According to NKVD figures that were released later on, around 700,000 officers and men of the Red Army deemed to have behaved with suspicion were detained in the first 10 months of the war by the blocking detachments. If there was a pressing need for them at the front, they were returned to active duty. Even so, around 10,000 were shot, frequently in the presence of their comrades. As the war went on, even the families of those deemed guilty of having surrendered in a state of panic were rounded up.

Detention was progressively replaced by harsher measures as the conflict unfolded. In September 1941, Zhukov, at the behest of Stalin, ordered machine guns to be turned on retreating battalions.

The punishment for simply being caught was particularly brutal and required significant manpower to carry out. On 27 December 1941 NKVD special camps were set up by the State Defence Committee, which between the previous June and October had ordered NKVD troops to detain some 650,000 who had retreated or left their units.

Not surprisingly, the creation of these blocking detachments aroused fierce resentment within the Red Army, and some troops dared to make their criticisms public. Their remarks ended up in NKVD files. Dissidents pointed out that there were occasions when the presence of the blocking detachments did nothing to help their side, as was pointed out by one complainant:

> These Blocking Detachments will shoot our soldiers from behind, the Germans from the front. As a result of this, there will be an armed confrontation between our units and the Blocking Detachments. The enemy will exploit this and may be able to smash us all...

Arrests and executions were often at the whim of scattered NKVD units. A past record of heroism could count for nothing. In one serious miscalculation, the NKVD ignored the dazzling record of Mikhail Petrovich Devyataev, which would have served as an invaluable blueprint for the Soviet fighting spirit and, more to the point, as an obvious recruiting model for the Red Air Force. Within months of the outbreak of war, Devyataev, from the impoverished Volga basin region of Mordovia, had flown 180 missions, engaged in sixteen dogfights, shot down eight enemy aircraft and received two wounds. One of these grounded him until he was able to wheedle his way back into a combat unit, only to be shot down by the Germans above Lvov.

All this was followed by incarceration and torture in the Sachsenhausen concentration camp, where by a miracle he escaped the gas chamber. He was then transferred to the camp at Svinemkonde on Uzedom Island in western Pomerania on the Baltic coast, a centre for the covert manufacture of V-1 and V-2 rockets. Here he and ten other prisoners were put to work shovelling snow on the airfield, where they succeeded in overpowering the crew and making off in a Heinkel bomber with Devyataev at the controls. A scrambled FW-190 fighter was successfully evaded and the stolen aircraft finally made its way back to the Soviet lines, armed with valuable information.

Much good did it do them. All were put into the hands of the NKVD. Their offence had been to allow themselves to be captured in the first place. The sentence for all was the GULAG, with release only after Stalin's death in 1953. It took another four years before Devyataev, 'politically rehabilitated', could become a Hero of the Soviet Union.

However, there were occasions when the Red Army had to step in and discipline NKVD formations. An incident in May 1942 was recalled by Alexander Yakovlev, a young marine, serving north of Moscow on the Volkov Front:

> One night our two battalions of marines were taken at the double through the darkness to a nearby village. We dug trenches and set up machine guns to cover a neighbouring wood. A division of NKVD troops – mostly conscripted policemen – who had broken at the Front, shortly emerged from the wood in disorder. Our Commissar, a man called Ksendz, told us to fire over their heads. He took a loudhailer and shouted at the fugitives to lie down. They did, and that of course stopped the panic. Ksendz was then able to sort them out into their platoons and companies, rally their officers, and send them back into the line. There were no casualties, but he told them the next time they panicked, the machine gunners would shoot to kill.

The NKVD sought to retain its power in Moscow. A vast shake-up of the security troops in and around the capital was instituted by Mikhail Zhuravlev, commander of the NKVD forces there. Out of town NKVD detachments and police joined the destroyer battalions. Realism, though, demanded that they should be under the command of the Red Army, which was in the position to supply the NKVD with the ammunition it lacked.

Hot on the German offensive against the Soviet Union, the NKVD was also involved in the arrest, deportation and execution of scores of Lithuanians, Poles and Belorussians, whom Stalin considered were likely to be German sympathisers or of dubious loyalty. The chaotic retreat of the Red Army during the early days of Barbarossa did not deter the despatch of trains of deportees and reprisals against those the Soviets had arrested. Among these were Lithuanians smarting under the Soviet Union's previous annexation and who took pride in the struggle for independence. As such they were arrested as 'enemies of the revolution'.

In Lithuania the NKVD, working with the Red Army, had tortured and mown down many in the western area of the Rainiai forest where victims had been held as prisoners in the town of Telsiai. Arrests and further killings occurred in surrounding villages, where inhabitants were held for owning a Lithuanian flag, possessing non-Communist literature and as landowners who had not surrendered their crops to the Soviet authorities.

Another killing ground was the town of Cherven, in the region of Minsk. Joanna Januszczak, a survivor who in June 1999 joined a reunion of former prisoners and relatives of victims of the NKVD, recalled how some 5,000 people had been crowded together and driven into exile and imprisonment in the east. She remembered:

> The women and most of those who had served time for criminal offences were separated from the crowd, while the others, political prisoners, were executed by NKVD firing squads. Those who remained alive after the firing were beaten to death with shovels. Only a few survived.

Among Poles who had managed to flee east from German-occupied areas were those who hoped for a sympathetic reception from the Russians. Many were to be severely disillusioned. Typical was the experience of the family of Abram Zeideman, who lived in the town of Gombin, with its predominantly Jewish population, situated some 90 miles west of Warsaw. In the spring of 1942, the Germans torched the Gombin synagogue and ghetto, carried out mass executions and despatched 212 surviving Jews to the extermination camp at Chelmno, lying south-west of Warsaw.

Zeideman and members of his family fled east, after being stopped several times by the Germans and pressed into work gangs. They and others eventually reached the town of Yanov, near Pinsk, where there were Jews who had also fled from Gombin and where Zeideman managed to get work as a tailor. But the Russian authorities gave them a choice: either he and his wife must accept Soviet citizenship, or they must register their intention to return to Poland. In his account of his experiences, Zeideman wrote:

> Owing to the fact that both my wife and I had relatives in Gombin we decided to register as Polish citizens desiring to go back. We registered and for a long time heard no more. Then, in the middle of the night we were awakened by a knock on the door. Several NKVD members entered, guns in hand, who told us to get dressed and accompany them. Permitted to take along a few personal belongings, we were led outside where a horse and wagon were waiting. Along with other refugees, we were ordered to climb into the wagon and were driven to the railroad station. We spent ten days and nights in airless, fetid, unsanitary carriages.
>
> The destination was Basharoya, a remote village to the south of the Archangelsk region of Siberia, surrounded by a thick forest where exiles were being held. The place consisted of several wooden barracks, subdivided into one room compartments, furnished with little iron beds and benches. Owing to the bright light, the worms and the insects crawled out of the walls, sleeping was out of the question.
>
> At dawn we were summoned to a meeting. There were several Russian families in our camp who took charge of us. At their head an NKVD official, Bayoff, who had an assistant named Samsonov. Bayoff greeted us with cold harsh words. 'You were not sent here for a certain period,' he said, 'you will remain here for ever. You declined to become citizens of the Soviet Union; you declined to accept Russian passports offered you; you are therefore traitors to the Fatherland. Those of you who want to live will have to work. All others will be buried here, under the firs. Here, in Russia, we firmly believe in the principle that he who does not work does not eat.' Many of those present began calling out their skills. One man declared he was a doctor, others called out they were

tailors, cobblers, tinsmiths. But the commander dismissed them all with a wave of the hand. 'Here', he said, 'you will forget what you were in the past. Here you will chop down trees.' As the work was being assigned, I was put in with a group of 'Drivers' whose task it was to haul the logs from the forest with horse and sled. The work was much more difficult than cutting wood in the forest, but the commandant promised us we would be better fed than the others. However, the difference between their portions and ours was 200 grams of black bread. The winter arrived early, bringing with it heavy snows and Arctic winds. Thus we worked and slaved in that distant, snowbound, God forsaken camp in the Siberian forest, removed from the rest of the world.

The Zeidemans remained in Russia either in imprisonment or on the run, dogged by the NKVD, until the war's end and beyond. The Poland to which they returned was, in Abram's words, 'a mass grave of our people'.

As for Dmitri Pavlov, deemed responsible for the earlier catastrophe of the Minsk pocket, he remained isolated in his Mogilev headquarters, an obvious target for the special sections. He was ordered to Moscow where his arrest, on charges of criminal incompetence and treason, was carried out by Mekhlis, while Beria's cohorts fulfilled their practised role of conducting interrogation and torture. It was later alleged that Pavlov and his associates had begged to be sent to the front as ordinary soldiers, to atone for the defeat of their armies. True or not, it made no difference. Sentences were passed against those accused of 'disgracing their rank, cowardice, lack of effectiveness, failure to manage troop control, abandoning weapons to the enemy without giving battle, and voluntarily quitting their military positions'. Pavlov was shot by firing squad, along with his chief of staff and three others.

Devious Abakumov

However, despite his ever-increasing authority, Beria was uneasy. He was forced to endure the baleful presence of the devious self-educated Muscovite Viktor Semyonovich Abakumov. Said to be the son of a hospital boilerman and a laundress, Abakumov's main loyalty was not to the Communist Party and the cause of social revolution, but strictly to his own interests: the attainment of power combined with a blatant pursuit of luxury and women. All three preoccupations were exploited simultaneously when he was working for OGPU, whose safe houses he used as centres for entertaining women, many of whom he subsequently employed as spies and detailed to gather evidence on those he was keen to denounce. What was termed 'disgraceful behaviour' had him demoted to GULAG guard. However, by the mid-1930s he had insinuated himself into the NKVD. Operating from a building opposite the Lubyanka, he installed listening equipment and made searches and arrests, going on to run border guards and uniformed police. As such he became invaluable to the special departments (OOs – *Osobyye Otdeli*) and, in the months before Barbarossa, he was made head of their department. The writer Aleksandr Solzhenitsyn, in his *The Gulag Archipelago*, revealed that Abakumov developed a taste for sadistic violence and torture of prisoners. ('He was not averse to taking a rubber truncheon in his hands once in a while.') Also serving within the special departments was Abakumov's deputy, M.D. Riumin, who, before conducting beatings, was said to be fastidious enough to ensure that the Persian carpet in his office was covered with an old, blood-bespattered strip of cloth.

Chapter 4

Birth of the Partisans

Throughout the summer of 1941, the NKVD monitored the stream of intelligence from areas considered under threat. There was increased focus on Leningrad, the former St Petersburg, northern gateway to Russia, key economic and cultural centre and, above all, cradle of revolution. The task of securing the Baltic and Leningrad was the task of Field Marshal Wilhelm Ritter von Leeb, commanding Army Group North. On 22 June, his forces in the area advanced to rip apart Soviet defences which were weakly organised and under-equipped. In less than a week, the people of Leningrad were mobilised to prepare defences. Men between the ages of sixteen and forty-five were deemed eligible for call up, while the city's unemployed were put to digging trenches for eight hours a day.

In the shadow of the impending siege, the NKVD exercised its authority both in the selection of border guards and internal security troops. NKVD 12th Border Guards were mustered just north of Memel, where the Germans crossed the frontier. They provided the sole defence against the enemy advance towards Palanga, in western Lithuania on the shore of the Baltic, key to the intended push up the Baltic coast. Within hours the border guards were reporting that Palanga was in flames, with battle raging in the streets. Extra manpower was mustered for the front line. Prisoners transported from labour camps were shoved into battle, prodded by the machine guns of the NKVD.

By early September, German forces were within 10 miles of Leningrad. The city's land communications were severed from the rest of Russia. Soon after the first German shells fell, the panzers reached the city's defences, to be followed by other forces who put a cordon across the south of Leningrad from the Gulf of Finland in the west to Lake Lagoda in the east. The Finns blocked the northern side of the city. By 9 September von Leeb was on the attack.

However, Hitler was becoming increasingly sensitive to the heavy demands on his forces who, in the face of booby traps and mines, were in danger of experiencing a high level of casualties. He preferred to subject Leningrad to bombardment, and, eventually, to weaken it by starvation. On 17 September, von Leeb's panzers switched to the south, while Army Group North, although weakened by earlier casualties, maintained the stranglehold close to the city.

Leningrad had to rely on dwindling supplies of heavy weapons and trained manpower. Subject to sustained bombing, the streets were soon lined with bodies. A witness, Vera Inbar, poet and writer, recorded:

> The mortuary itself is full. Not only are there too few trucks
> to go the cemetery, but more important, not enough gasoline
> to put in the trucks and the main thing is – there is not enough
> strength left in the living to bury the dead.

Zhukov appointment

The blame for Leningrad's plight was pinned on Marshal Klimont Voroshilov, who was in command of the armed forces in the area. It was said he had failed to anticipate the German plan to besiege the city. The need for drastic action was apparent. Stalin turned to Zhukov, his Chief of the General Staff. Zhukov had climbed the career ladder fast, gaining the attention and respect of Stalin. He displayed both his leader's notorious coarseness and total lack of scruple in demanding action. On 8 September, Zhukov flew into Leningrad from Moscow with the order from Stalin to take control.

Zhukov began working with two close colleagues: Andrei Zhdanov, the Leningrad Party Secretary and effective supremo of Leningrad, and Vsevolod Merkulov, the Caucasian Russian who was the Deputy People's Commissar of the NKVD. Merkulov's prime concern was weak discipline within the Red Army. There were growing reports of troops deserting and fleeing in panic. An order was issued to stem the flow of 'anti-Soviet agitation, desertion and the penetration of enemy elements'. Agitation was interpreted by the NKVD in the widest terms, including soldier's protests about working conditions and even complaints of food shortages. To implement Merkulov's requirements, operations staff drew on NKVD personnel from the security directorate, the rear services of the Northern Front and the headquarters of 2nd NKVD Division. They were required to increase the number of patrols of the city's main streets and key installations.

Bridgehead failure

Zhukov's deep-seated arrogance tended to alienate him from those with whom he worked, not least members of the NKVD. His callous indifference to the high volume of casualties also shocked many. Typical was his determination to launch a number of massed attacks on the Germans from a minuscule foothold on the Nevsky bridgehead, on the eastern bank of the Neva river, part of which flowed through the heart of Leningrad. To the west of the tip of the Neva, the Germans held a narrow defence corridor. It was vital that they be prevented from crossing the river. Following a reconnaissance, on 12 September Zhukov ordered a night-time landing on the Neva's far bank with a scratch force of NKVD border guards, a brigade of marines and a regular infantry division to take the bridgehead.

Ordered to cross the Neva to pick up supplies and equipment, the men found that there were no boats available and they were required to construct their own rafts. Since these were likely to be weighed down with double the regulation load of ammunition and grenades, progress was agonisingly slow. Mikhail Pavlov, a colonel in the 1st NKVD Border Guards, recorded:

> It was dark, but as we approached the far bank, the enemy found his range and the water was rocked by explosions – our ammunition was blowing up around us. Our guys on the rafts were sitting ducks – we lost an entire battalion during the crossing.

The Germans dug in, reinforcing their position around the small

Soviet enclave. Although the Nevsky bridgehead was a virtual death trap, this did not persuade Zhukov to evacuate. Deaf to all pleas, he pushed in still more troops. But by then it was apparent that this first attempt to break a German blockade had failed. In his own defence, Zhukov argued that the Nevsky bridgehead had been vital for the city's survival. A backup of a Red Army detachment proved useless. The force on the bridgehead, trapped by overwhelming German artillery fire, was powerless to move.

On the outskirts of Leningrad, German forces had advanced steadily during August, their infantry aided by formidable tank muscle, overcoming resistance as they breached the Soviet-held lines. Then, within striking distance of the village of Petrozavodsk, came a mighty obstacle, packed into the sturdy frame of Junior Lieutenant Alexandr Andreyevich Divochkin, a native of the village of Lopatino near Moscow. He had been aged 27 at the start of the Great Patriotic War and now commanded a battery of the 15th Motorised Infantry Regiment of the NKVD. Furious fighting erupted and with it signs of disaster: the artillery teams holding back the Germans were knocked out. Divochkin, galvanised, streaked from cover to cover in a bid to assess a rapidly deteriorating defensive situation, the Germans shelling with everything they had.

When his commander fell it was all down to Divochkin. When a shell exploded in the boxes of artillery ammunition, starting a fire, his life was at risk as he smothered the flames with sand, positioning his gun and letting loose. Amid the merciless barrage of shells he kept on firing, then ran to another gun and fired that too, successfully giving the illusion that the Soviet position was intact.

For two gruelling hours Divochkin gave orders, ceaselessly working the two guns, only too aware that the Germans were within grenade-throwing distance. Thankfully, the Soviet contingents had been able to regroup and muster a counter-attack. All the while, Divochkin kept up his firing in support of his troops. When it was all over, some 70 dead Germans were counted, while many more were wounded and left on the battlefield. Many heavy machine guns were captured. On 26 August 1941, Junior Lieutenant Divochkin became a Hero of the Soviet Union, one of the earliest recipients of this honour of the war.

As for the situation in Moscow, forces engaged in the drive there encountered direct intervention by Hitler at the end of July. The Führer, who had never regarded the capital as the Russian nerve centre, issued an order from Armed Forces Headquarters on 21 August declaring 'The essential target to be achieved before winter is not the capture of Moscow but the conquest of the Crimea and the Donets coal and industrial basin.' Hitler also had his attention fixed on Kiev, capital of the Ukraine, with its rich oil and industrial resources. Guderian protested that a concerted thrust could well put Moscow at Hitler's feet. This was ignored and the Führer insisted that the advance on Moscow could only be undertaken after the fall of Kiev. This was achieved on 19 September amid awful carnage and a claim by the Germans to have captured 655,000 prisoners, one third of the total strength of the Red Army.

'Last great battle'

Only now was Hitler prepared to turn his attention to Moscow, confident of what he declared would be 'the last – the great – battle'. It was launched on 2 October as Operation *Taifun* (Typhoon). Field Marshal Gerd von Rundstedt, Commander of Army Group South, who had taken part in the capture of Kiev, pressed eastward to capture Kharkov, the USSR's fourth-largest city and a vital rail junction, and from there progressed to Rostov, at the mouth of the Don. Troops of the Soviet 38th Army, reinforced by 47th NKVD Rifle Brigade, carried out a number of successful counter-attacks in the area.

Sergei Kruglov, a hulking fresh-faced peasant and former tank mechanic with an impeccable record as a Chekist who had joined the NKVD two years before, was put to work organising the penal system of forced labour camps that embodied the GULAG. In the days of Nikolai Yezhov, the camps had been centres of repression, relying on forced labour and involving large-scale construction of roads, railways and waterways. Repression continued after the German invasion but became more selective. In place of wholesale slaughter, prisoners' special abilities were harnessed: scientists were mustered to a special prison at Bolshevo, outside Moscow, and provided with appropriate facilities. The GULAG population itself declined sharply. By the summer of 1944, some of the worst months for the Nazis, some 6.5 million Soviet troops were facing the Germans – of which more than one million had been transferred to the Red Army from the GULAG.

Meanwhile, in response to the German advance, defensive lines had been built around Moscow, concentrating initially on the Nara river outside the city, and along the inner and outer boulevards. The capital experienced the grip of terror, with German aircraft bombing and strafing, while looters scoured the empty apartments of those tens of thousands who had made for the choked stations to join the last of the eastbound trains.

Beria obstructive

There were numerous occasions when the exasperated Red Army clashed with the NKVD, which it regarded as deliberately obstructive. Interventions came from Beria, often without notice, questioning the value of the intelligence he received. A particular incident involved Colonel N.A. Sbytov of the Moscow Military District, who received a report from two reconnaissance pilots that a formidable motorised and armoured formation was threatening Yukhnov, lying to the south of Moscow. Preparations were already well in hand to confront the German columns when Beria made an unexpected telephone call, insisting that the information had come from 'nonsense' sources, involving 'panic mongers and saboteurs'. He had the support of Abakumov, who demanded photographic proof of the pilots' claim. In some heat, Sbytov declared that such proof did not exist and stressed the value of the pilots' observations.

Abakumov's reaction was to threaten Sbytov with a military tribunal, a move opposed both by the military district and the Party's Central Committee. After considerable wranglings, Beria and Abakumov were sharply overruled. The legacy of the incident was contempt for the NKVD. More seriously at this time there were claims that the NKVD had disarmed Red Army troops fighting their way out of enemy encirclement. Unarmed and defenceless, the troops were trapped again by the Germans, who mowed them down.

Beria's self-proclaimed rear security units, which employed machine-gunners to keep troops from any unauthorised withdrawals, were widely regarded as needlessly obstructive. Red Army leaders declared that they were quite capable of maintaining discipline themselves. It made little difference. When a broadcast report revealed that, during the night of 14–15 October, the position on the western front had worsened, with German tanks breaking through defences, NKVD divisions were forthwith assigned an extra role.

Two of these elite divisions, the 9th Dzerzhinsky Division tasked to prevent enemy mechanised units breaking through, and the 2nd NKVD Motor Rifle Division, assigned to cover the Moscow approaches from the north and north-east, were expected to open fire on any retreating troops. Other functions involved street patrols, guarding public buildings and arresting saboteurs, as well as detaining those criticising the state, or spreading what were deemed to be panic and rumours. Their ranks were supplemented by home defence units, termed 'destroyer battalions', whose duties involved rooting out looters and deserters and killing enemy parachutists.

The threat of panic was ever present. Lieutenant Vladimir Ogryzko of state security, aged twenty-four at the time and a commander of an NKVD detachment, in a television interview in 1999, spoke of:

> ...diversionary groups and spies who had broken through Moscow's defences... There were robberies – everything you can imagine happened – because as usual the people lost their heads... the ill-educated ones. The scum of the earth did show its face. It seeped through.

Those attempting to flee by car had their vehicles bulldozed. Ogryzko added: 'If the driver was crushed, well, even better'.

Over his own signature, Stalin issued a decree:

> ...for the purposes of securing the defence of Moscow... and also for the purpose of terminating the undermining activities of spies, diversionists and other agents of German fascism, all agents of the enemy, apprehended for disturbing law and order must be shot on the spot.

At the same time, draconian powers were given to Major General Sinilov, the Moscow city commandant who had at his disposal the NKVD troops responsible for the capital's internal defence, including the arrest and execution of anyone fleeing from the advancing Germans or deserting. Those that were caught and rounded up appeared before military tribunals working around the clock.

Growth of partisans

Despite all the efforts of the Kremlin, partisans operating behind the German lines were prone to insubordination, were poorly organised and were notorious for ignoring orders. Beria, conscious as usual that any shortcomings could well rebound on him, outlined to Stalin proposals for drastic reorganisation of his men by forming highly disciplined partisan detachments, able to commit effective sabotage while providing the Red Army with useful intelligence. He received the go-ahead and by early August 1941 was able to inform Stalin that partisan detachments had been formed from NKVD units in all regions along the western front.

The growth from there was fast. In the Ukraine alone three fully armed partisan detachments were formed, numbering 1,000–2,000 men each. It was just the start. By late 1942, partisans had edged even more closely into the Soviet intelligence network with a formal chain of command able to supply both the Red Army and the NKVD command with military, political and economic intelligence. Undercover agents were infiltrated into regions that the Germans were having difficulty in controlling. Notable were the Pripet Marshes, the vast area of swamp and bogland lying south-west of Moscow, which only those with local knowledge could penetrate effectively. There were occasions when this was a crucial advantage in the face of an enemy often better armed and equipped.

The NKVD also introduced the newly styled Administration for Special Tasks, which was put in overall control of the partisan detachments. According to where they were called upon to operate, the partisans could find themselves up against more than just Germans. The Ukraine, in particular, proved to be a melting pot of loyalties. For instance, thousands of Ukrainians were anti-Communists, seeking liberation from the Soviet Union by joining the UPA, the military arm of the Ukrainian nationalists, guerrillas who fought at battalion strength, slaughtering Jews as well as pro-Soviet Ukrainians. These partisans, led by Sydor Kovpak, himself a Ukrainian and a survivor of the purges, fought in the Carpathian mountains against nationalists as well as the Germans.

Elsewhere, targets were more easily defined: German supply trains were derailed and blown up with mines. Fyodr Alexeyevich Malyshev, from the eastern Gomel region of Belorussia, was a mechanical engineer whose speciality had been building labour-saving detachments, but he was soon filling a rather different role.

His talents were badly needed. On 11 July 1941, in a rapid advance, the enemy had seized Vitenex, to the north-east of Belorussia, unleashing a regime of persecution, forced labour and murder. On the pretext that epidemics were raging within the ghetto where 16,000 Jews had eventually settled, the Germans went on a three-day killing spree during which the victims were dragged to the Bitbe River, where they were shot and their bodies flung into the water. Elsewhere, special trains transported prisoners to concentration camps. Attention centred on the Brest-Gomel railway line, the critical transport artery for German Army Group Centre. Malyshev's unit worked tirelessly to destroy it, planting the explosives under the tracks. On one occasion, villagers blocked the view of the guards as Malyshev removed a mine from under his shirt, then ran down the embankment at the approach of the train.

In the records of the 125th Partisan Brigade, one typical operation was described:

> An enemy troop train consisting of 60 carriages was blown up today. All traffic in that section of the railways was stopped for two days and nights. The Nazis cordoned off the area where the train had been derailed, and were engaged for 36 hours in carrying out their dead, dismantling the smashed carriages, and clearing the track. The train had been carrying an anti-Partisan punitive detachment.

By November 1942 Malyshev had been responsible for destroying sixteen trains, a success rate that led to his appointment as leader of a demolition squad. In a desperate bid to keep the railway lines open, the Germans hunted the partisans day and night and it became increasingly difficult to continue to derail the trains. But the pressure was maintained, causing considerable damage to the Germans active in Belorussia.

Chocolates to kill

As for the Administration for Special Tasks, it was headed by a fiercely dedicated Ukrainian, Pavel Sudoplatov, who had joined the Cheka at the age of fourteen and had speedily gained promotion to the Secret Political Department of the local OGPU. Here he had networked tirelessly, seeking a meeting with Emma Kaganova, from Gomel, Belorussia, a senior colleague and a wise choice as wife because she eventually ensured his promotion.

In 1992, four years before Sudoplatov's death, two writers, Jerrold L. and Leona P. Schecter, helped him, at the age of 85, prepare his memoirs, entitled, appropriately enough, *Special Tasks*. His narrative revealed how sabotage operations had been carried out behind enemy lines before and during the war with a formidable array of assassinations, sabotage and guerrilla killings. During the Spanish Civil War he had posed as a Polish volunteer on the Republican side, cover for his true allegiance to a guerilla warfare group run by the NKVD. As well as involvement in the killing of Trotsky, Sudoplatov revealed how he had been one of some half-dozen highly skilled agents prepared to go out and kill. In the summer of 1938, on the eve of the Second World War, a particular target was Yevhen Konovalets, whose organisation supported a Ukrainian- German alliance, raising fears in the Kremlin that this would lead to progressive penetration of the Soviet Union. On Stalin's orders, Sudoplatov contacted Konovalets, pretending to be a sympathiser.

A plan had been concocted, centring on Konovalets's well-known weakness for chocolates. The two men had agreed to get together in Rotterdam. The NKVD's technical bureau had been ordered to create a bomb disguised as a box of chocolates, on the outside cover of which was a traditional Ukrainian decoration. On Sudoplatov's plea of shortage of time, the two men fixed a brief meeting that evening at the Atlanta restaurant. Sudoplatov recalled: 'I laid the box near him on the table in a horizontal position. We shook hands and I left, carefully controlling my desire to run. I heard a bang that sounded like the blow out of a tyre. People were running towards the restaurant. I hurried to the railway station and boarded the first train to Paris.' The bomb, meanwhile, had exploded in Konovalets's face and killed him. It was an execution dictated by the needs of war rather than paying off old scores.

Sudoplatov and the administration then shifted emphasis by instigating a rigid training programme for saboteurs and partisans, one situated in a former rest home south of Moscow, while the other was at Kuntsevo, near Stalin's dacha on the city's western outskirts. Recruits learnt classic guerilla tactics, with the emphasis on speed. Once strategic targets had been earmarked and attacked, the partisans melted away into the night; pursuit in forests or marshland was virtually impossible.

Despite the achievements of the partisans, the advance on Moscow by General Hoth's Panzer Group 3 and 9th Army was unstoppable. The decision was made in October 1941 to shift the seat of government to the city of Kuybyshev, due east of the capital, while Stalin and the Stavka stayed behind. Beria moved his office from the Lubyanka to the basement of No.2 Dzerzhinsky Street, which had its own air-raid shelter.

As well as recognising the urgent need to defend the capital, Beria was all too soon sucked into the deep-seated squabble between his NKVD troops and their co-controllers, the General Staff of the Red Army, who were directing manoeuvres at the front. In addition, the move to Kuybyshev gave the NKVD the excuse to be rid of a number of prisoners. Some victims were murdered in their cells, while others were shot without trial, accused by Beria of being members of anti-Soviet, Trotskyite organisations.

At this time, the Soviet Union was facing a severe threat. By 14 October 1941, Hoth's troops crossed the Volga at Kalinin (later Tver) cutting the Moscow-Leningrad railway and bringing the German forces close to the northern outskirts of Moscow. NKVD internal troops aided the evacuation of key armaments factories to the east, while offices and businesses which could not be evacuated were blown up. The Commissariat of Armaments and Munitions, the department concerned with the production of weapons of war, was effectively controlled by Beria, and he used NKVD prisoners as forced labour. It was later revealed that 448,000 of these prisoners were detailed for railway construction. NKVD labour was also used extensively for the mining of coal and metals for purposes of defence.

Beria's methods of getting his own way remained unchanged, as was pointed out by Victor Kravchenko, an engineer in the defence industry and a later defector, who wrote: 'The nominal Commissars... would have preferred a quick death to the righteous anger of Beria and his organisation. Everyone in the plants and offices and institutions directly or indirectly connected with armaments and munitions was gripped by dread fear. Beria was no engineer. He was placed in control for the precise purpose of inspiring deadly fear.'

At this time, fear of Beria was not confined to the factory floor. He had long been the subject of allegations that he was addicted to seducing and raping young women. At night, it was attested that he prowled streets in his official armoured limousine, ordering his driver to stop, seize a likely prospect and throw her into the back of the car. Rape was said to take place in Beria's own quarters on occasion. Recent accounts of his life have tended to treat these allegations with caution. Such claims were embellished by Beria's former opponents following his removal from office and subsequent execution in 1953.

Although rumours about Beria's behaviour could not have failed to reach Stalin, at that time the Soviet leader had more pressing concerns. Early in October, Zhukov had received a telegram ordering him to return to Moscow. Stalin confined his interest in Leningrad to asking whether it could hold out, before despatching Zhukov to travel to the Moscow sector of the front line, where he encountered chaos within the various military formations around the city.

State of siege

The forces situated before Moscow came under Zhukov, whose resources at that time were not nearly enough to prevent a German breakthrough. As a succession of towns and villages fell, Moscow prepared for siege. Apartment buildings were evacuated and turned into strong-points, and workers and peasants were mobilised along with office and factory staffs. Buildings, material and transport were commandeered. Spades, axes, picks and crowbars were supplied to some 600,000 Muscovites, while those who were able-bodied and aged 18 or over were mustered for forced labour and the building of defences.

Intelligence briefings, supplied by his well-placed agents, reached Sergei Fedoseyev, head of the Moscow region's counter-intelligence section, revealing that Otto Skorzeny, a highly-regarded SS officer, had been entrusted with securing key Communist buildings in the city, including the Lubyanka and the Central Telegraph. The myth arose that Moscow was unassailable, thanks to the presence of an impregnable stern and resolute Red Army. The truth was very different. Moscow was a city gripped by fear. Secret Document No.34, of the State Defence Committee, dated 15 October 1941, showed that a decision had been taken to:

> ...evacuate the Presidium of the Supreme Soviet and the top levels of government... In the event of enemy forces arriving at the gates of Moscow, the NKVD – Comrade Beria and Comrade Scherbakov – are ordered to blow up the business premises, warehouses and installations which cannot be evacuated, and all of the Underground electrical equipment, along with major cultural and historic sites, so as to deprive them from the invading Germans.

Alexsandr Bogomolov, a long-time member of the Special Motorised Brigade (*Omsbonovtsevi*, OMSBONO), of the NKVD, responsible to the NKVD's Fourth Directorate, had been among those assigned to handle these 'special tasks'. During October, at the time of the government's declaration of a state of siege, he joined an eight-man team of demolition experts. They were trained to plant explosives in major hotels, the Cathedral of the Epiphany, the Bolshoi Theatre's orchestra pit, Stalin's dacha and the Livadia Palace in the Crimean city at Yalta. Owners were to be forcibly ejected from private homes and apartments which were taken over by the NKVD, converted to wireless stations or used as sites known as 'dead drops' for placing secret items such as instructions, codes and maps.

Camouflage and sandbags

Because of natural and man-made landmarks around Moscow, it was reasoned that Luftwaffe pilots would have little difficulty in identifying key targets. So the NKVD appointed two special commissions to discover ways of camouflaging, among others, the Kremlin and the Lenin Mausoleum. While the latter was sandbagged and wreathed with netting, the walls of the Kremlin were repainted to resemble house fronts, while major roads were covered to appear as roof tops. As well as disguising vital factories, bogus ones were fashioned out of wood and cardboard.

Women and children were put to digging ditches, constructing tank traps and primitive barricades. Stavka deployed six tired Soviet armies, under-strength in numbers and weapons. Worst of all, it emerged that Zhukov could only call on 500 light tanks. Serious setbacks were the loss of the cities of Kalinin to the north of Moscow and Kaluga to the south.

Inevitably, news of Zhukov's plight could not be concealed from anxious Muscovites. But anyone overheard by the NKVD expressing the belief that the capital would be overrun and that the Soviet Union should sue for peace, was arrested on a charge of spreading 'anti-revolutionary rumours'. These could be interpreted in any way that the courts directed, not least as criticism of Stalin and the policies of the government. Sentences of a minimum ten years imprisonment handed out by the Peoples' Courts became mandatory.

Early in 1941 there were also changes within the security machinery, with increased power afforded to both Viktor Abakumov and Vsevolod Merkulov, the latter becoming commissar within the newly-formed NKGB. Abakumov assumed the post of counter-intelligence chief, directly responsible to Beria.

Vassily Grossman, a prominent and highly outspoken Soviet-era writer and war reporter, whose diaries, notebooks and personal correspondence have been edited and translated by Antony Beevor and Luba Vinogradova, showed that, despite increased threats against any semblance of criticism, some individuals were prepared to be perceptive and honest eye-witnesses in the front line. Grossman, writing for the newspaper *Krasnaya Zveda*, The Red Star, revealed the uncomfortable truth that not all men were going into battle with the ecstatic urge to die for Stalin. There were badly wounded troops who, while in hospital, had to endure the indignity of being subjected to checks by the NKVD, whose agents were forever suspicious that the wounds had been self-inflicted. There were also cases of Red Army surgeons who, at great personal risk, dared to safeguard the lives of patients who claimed to have been severely injured in battle. Grossman's writings brought him into dispute with the higher reaches of the NKVD and could easily have landed him in the GULAG.

By early October, both protagonists faced the twin threat of autumn mud and, unseasonably early, the first falls of snow. This was the *rasputitsa* ('quagmire season'), when large reaches of flat lands and non-paved roads became muddy and marshy. On the German side, General Hans von Greiffenburg, Chief of Staff of the 12th Army, declared: 'The effect of climate in Russia is to make things impassable in the mud of spring and autumn, unbearable in the heat of summer and impossible in the depths of winter. Climate in Russia is a series of natural disasters.' Indeed, the ill-equipped Germans suffered the most. Their men lacked warm protective clothing, while there was no strong line of field fortifications into which their army might retire. In no way was Hitler prepared to tolerate a halt in his advance. In the circumstances, sustained progress became virtually impossible.

However, on the Soviet side in Leningrad, military operations did not come to a standstill. For example, soldiers of the 1st Rifle Division of the NKVD were employed to eliminate German penetration within the rail station of Mga in the north-west. A squadron headed by battalion commander A. Pyankov not only saw off the Germans, but also, while facing two enemy regiments, seized around 150 enemy motor vehicles, only withdrawing as losses mounted.

Red Square parade

Reports had been reaching Stalin that German prisoners had been boasting to their captors that it would be the triumphant Wehrmacht who would be parading in Red Square on 7 November 1941, the anniversary of the Russian Revolution. To Stalin there could only be one riposte: he declared that the Soviet parade would be held as usual. There was consternation from his generals, who thought it would provide an opportunity for the Germans to attack on a horrific scale. Stalin overruled all these reservations, despite the German advance.

The organisation of the parade was overseen by the NKVD, whose leaders insisted that the decision to hold a parade should be an official secret for as long as possible. Beria did not take long to assign a role for himself, ushering in regiments of his troops to make sure the streets were free of riff-raff and looters ahead of the event. Many of the troops who were to take part were conscripts with no experience of parades and they needed time to practice. They were taken off battle exercises and were put through up to four hours of specialised drill each day. The Dzerzhinski Division's military band was mustered to teach the recruits to march to music.

Amid gathering falls of snow, the parade, launched by eight chiming Kremlin bells and led by Marshal Semyn Budyenny on a white charger, was pure theatre. It was covered by newsreel cameramen and accompanied by a rousing commentary and a speech on radio by Stalin, transmitted far beyond Moscow. The result was a triumphant gamble, an incalculable boost to Russian morale. But there was still a war to be fought. When the parade was over the troops who had taken part marched from Red Square back to the front.

At the same time, renewed attention had been focused on Leningrad, where, following Hitler's deliberate policy, battle had given way to siege. By September three million inhabitants had been trapped by the Germans. During that winter, enemy shelling reduced the roads to ice-filled craters, while rubble and rubbish lay uncleared in the streets. Targets from the air were food stores, power-plants and waterworks. The NKVD imposed a strict curfew; those found on the streets outside designated hours were swiftly arrested as suspected enemy agents. Photography was forbidden, and anyone found with a camera became subject to punishment under military law, which could mean the firing squad.

For some Leningraders, this was not their first encounter with repression. Four years earlier, the Central Committee of the Politburo had announced that it was undertaking a large-scale 'operation for the repression of former kulaks, active anti-Soviet elements and criminals.' The Leningrad NKVD Directorate had received a copy of a Secret Administrative Order for immediate implementation which resulted, during the remaining pre-war years, in the slaughter of 4,000 people and the imprisonment of another 10,000. Simultaneously, a mass campaign against 'spies and saboteurs' had been ongoing. The arrests had been undertaken by the instigators of the purges, operating at the whim of an increasingly paranoid Stalin.

Olga Berggolts

Among the victims was the family of Olga Fyodorovna Berggolts, a widely-respected poet, writer and journalist. It has been said that her arrest was ordered by Stalin because her surname sounded suspiciously German. Pregnant with a child destined to be stillborn in the Leningrad NKVD prison, she underwent interrogations 'focused on breaking my will and messing with my soul, trying to degrade my life by making me feel helpless and hopeless'. No evidence of disloyalty could be found and she was eventually released. But freedom came with conditions. She was to use her professional skills to lift the spirits of a besieged city. Her work was in radio where, with her calming voice, she built up a large audience, both with news bulletins from the front line and with recitals of her own prose and poetry.

It was a hard enough task to lift spirits amid an atmosphere of widespread despair. Privations were so appalling that for sheer survival people ate their pets and many also ate their dead. There were instances of administrative muddle with supplies of food not getting through. By the start of October, there was sufficient food for just 20 days, and by 1 November, only enough for a week. When the waters of Lake Lagoda had frozen over sufficiently, trucks were able to carry some food across what became known as the 'Ice Road' or the 'Road of Life'. Progress was slow, the volume of supplies only improving under the ruthless direction of Andrei Zhdanov and Admiral Nikolai Kuznetsov, Stavka's Leningrad representative, who sacked incompetent managers and cajoled, bullied and harassed the truck drivers, while simultaneously bribing them with bonuses. There were instances of trucks being hijacked by bands who promptly proceeded to sell the contents on the black market. Those that were caught were turned over to the NKVD. New problems came with the spring thaw of 1942 when Leningrad became cursed with epidemics, spread not least by thousands of unburied putrid corpses. Bands were set to work cleaning up the city.

By contrast, winter in Moscow had proved the capital's saviour. Troops mustered from Siberia to the Russian front had been far better equipped to withstand the bitter cold. Crucially, many of the Wehrmacht's weapons had not been adapted to the change of climate and did not function well. The progress of German forces had been too slow. The initiative belonged to Zhukov, whose men moved in for the kill, intent on encircling Army Group Centre. No quarter was given. An example of Zhukov's ruthlessness was his use of men in dark clothing, who had been press-ganged from punishment battalions to lead white-camouflaged troops into battle. Anyone from these battalions who fled to the rear was shot out of hand.

It was the turn of the German armies to become fragmented and disorganised. Supplies of fuel, both for transport and cooking, dwindled. Frostbite raged, with thousands of its victims needing amputation. Zhukov's ruthless steamroller was deemed to have achieved its purpose; on 8 December 1941, Hitler accepted the need to call off the Moscow offensive. By the end of the month, all the territory lost since the previous October had been recaptured by the Russians.

As for Beria, one of his main concerns was to solve the problem of prisoners who were still rotting in Soviet jails. The logistics of transporting them to the country's interior proved complicated; the easier way out was through a succession of purges. In all 157 prominent prisoners were shot.

Beria's desire for revenge had long been smouldering. Prisoners were condemned as members of organisations that were 'anti-Soviet and Trotskyite'. A prominent figure among those was 30–year–old air force Lieutenant General Pavel Rychagov, previously regarded as a glamourous figure and a favourite of Stalin, who had flown in the Winter War in Finland and during the Spanish Civil War. The fact that he was a Hero of the Soviet Union and holder of a second Order of Lenin ultimately availed him nothing. At a conference he dared to challenge Stalin face-to-face after the latter had criticised the air force for a high accident rate. Rychagov retorted with some heat that Stalin was to blame for tolerating too many 'flying coffins'. It was enough to seal his fate. He was arrested by the NKVD and shot.

However, the halt of the German armies before Moscow had given them one useful advantage. They had been able to regroup and to established bases, such as the major towns of Demyansk, Orel and Kursk, which had been insufficiently fortified during the advances of the previous year.

Agony of Kharkov

Stalin's primary objective was to recapture Kharkov. On 12 May, Soviet troops managed to break through the German defences to the north and south of the city. But here the Germans were ready for them and the Russians were routed. Soviet forces in sight of Kharkov were then ordered to break off, turn south and stem the German advance. But the Russian armies were trapped; some 70,000 of their soldiers were killed and another 200,000 captured. Further south, a bid to drive the Germans out of the Crimea also failed. During June, the heavily fortified city of Sevastopol on the edge of the Black Sea was battered into ruins.

Fortune, for the moment, remained on the side of the Germans whose forces, along with their Hungarian, Italian and Romanian allies, shielded by aircraft and tanks, pushed ahead, reaching the River Don. German troops, in the wake of the powerful armour, reached Rostov, gateway to the Caucasus. Here fanatical units of the NKVD had turned the city into a giant death trap, their machine-gunners sited on the Taganrog road leading to the bridge. Streets were a massive tangle of barricades; houses became arsenals. For 50 hours, German assault troops fought ferociously.

By dawn on 25 July Russian units had fallen back in confusion beyond the Don. It was later claimed that they had failed to put up sufficient fight, and there were accounts of men wounding themselves and discarding their weapons. For once indiscipline had been overlooked by a dispirited NKVD, although many soldiers had fought to the death. In a bid to stem any further decline, Stalin issued 'Order 227 Not A Step Back! (*Ni Shagu Nazad!*), declaring:

> Each position, each metre of Soviet territory must be stubbornly defended, to the last drop of blood. We must cling to every inch of Soviet soil and defend it to the end... From now on, the iron law of discipline for every commander, Red Army soldier and political worker must be the demand – not a step backwards without the order of a superior commander.

The Caucasus

Hitler, in a burst of self-confidence, had split his forces in two. One section would push across the Don to Stalingrad, while the other would head southward towards what became the Führer's obsession: seizing Russia's oil-rich Caucasus. This was a mountain-barrier region, sited between the two continents of Europe and Asia, comprising areas of Georgia, Armenia, Azerbaijan and Chechnya. Directive 41 (otherwise Operation Blue, *Blau*), aimed 'to wipe out the entire defence potential remaining to the Soviets'.

Although outwardly phelgmatic, Stalin nursed a secret fear. This was centred on his native Georgia, of whose history he was acutely conscious. In 1917, an anti-Bolshevik Transcaucasian Federation had been established between Azerbaijan and Armenia, which the Soviet Union subsequently annexed. In 1936, Georgia had become a separate Soviet republic, but its loyalty to Soviet Russia could not be taken entirely for granted. Another concern was the stance of adjacent Turkey and its links with the Turkic peoples, a broadly based, ethno-linguistic group whose Muslims were considered to be the most sympathetic to the German cause.

There was plainly a need for intervention. Beria, whose Georgian background was an advantage, was despatched in late August by Stalin to the Trans-Caucasus Front, accompanied by a posse of NKVD associates. The demand from the front had been that the fresh troops should be from the Red Army. Beria's reaction displayed boundless arrogance; he claimed that he was representing Stavka and incurred the fury of I.V. Tiulenev, the Trans-Caucasian front commander, who declared that Beria and one of his colleagues, Bogdan Kobulov, had assumed an authority to which they were not entitled. When Tiulenev requested of Stalin that he should have command of a certain number of NKVD troops transferred to him, Beria erupted in fury, but finally lost out when Stalin agreed. Tiulenev later alleged that:

> Throughout his brief stay at the front, Beria did not once display a serious interest in the defence system elaborated by the Military Council of the front and approved by the Stavka... Beria's trips to the defence lines in the area of Makhachkala, Groznyi, Vladikavkaz and Sukhumi boiled down to showiness and noise, to the creation of a façade of concern about the organisation and strengthening of defence. In fact with his criminal attitude and conduct he only disorganised, hindered and disrupted our work.

The fact that he had what he considered to be a free hand from Stalin had gone to Beria's head and the situation had all the makings of a major disaster. As ever interested solely in extending his power, he had set about organising a parallel NKVD force to oversee the defence of the entire North Caucasus, where the Germans were concentrating on the area's mountain passes. Beria's dream of an NKVD-manned Caucasus Range Operational Group led by himself was sheer fantasy; the passes would be scaled by crack troops from the elite German LXXIX Jäger Corps who were well equipped for mountain combat. Stalin was alerted; the idea of a Caucasus Range Operational Group was swiftly aborted.

Mass murder

During this period, the NKVD rear-area security and interior troops continued their programme of mass murder against communities thought to be sympathetic to the Germans. Action was particularly brutal towards the Volga Autonomous Republic, containing many ethnic Germans. These were Russians of German descent who had settled on the reaches of the Volga River many centuries before. Hatreds went back to the days of the Russian Civil War, when Volga German communities had clashed with the Red Army. In the Second World War, Stalin's wholesale condemnation of all Germans as enemies of the state led to a formal Decree of Banishment. This abolished the autonomous republic and was followed by the exile, internment or deportment to western Siberia of some 600,000 'wreckers and spies'.

Confident of his power within the Caucasus, Beria switched to long-mooted plans for the deportation of entire ethnic groups, who had collaborated with the Germans in order to avenge the tyranny they suffered under Stalin. Among these were the Kabarda–Balkaria Autonomous Soviet Socialist Republic of North Caucasus, many of whose inhabitants willingly provided advancing German troops with valuable intelligence and mustered forces to clash with retreating Soviet formations and smaller units. Self-defence troops were on hand to hold the impressive number of mountain villages and maintain security in occupied areas. Fierce retaliation came from the Soviet 37th Army, whose commander ordered the destruction of entire Balkar villages.

An order was passed to Colonel Shikin of 11th NKVD Rifle Division whose troops, under Captain Nakin, stormed seven villages on 28 November, slaughtering some 700 inhabitants. Similar measures were taken elsewhere in the region by other NKVD units, including Ordzhonikidze Rifle Division and Grozny Rifle Division of Home Security troops.

On the battle fronts, German fortunes seemed to be at their peak. With the break of dawn over the plains of southern Russia on 23 August 1942, tanks of 16th Panzer Division, spearheading General Friedrich Paulus's 6th Army, had seemed unstoppable as they crossed the Don with Stalingrad a mere 40 miles to the east. To the south, von Kleist's First Panzer Army was also advancing rapidly. Von Kleist was unaware that the NKVD was using forced labour to slave day and night to dig defences for key cities and mountain passes. By the beginning of autumn about 100,000 defensive works had been completed, with some 70,000 pillboxes and firing points and 1,600km of trenches blocking the German advance.

Chapter 5

'Not One Step Back'

The NKVD, despite its determination to hang on to every shred of power, had, as events in Stalingrad unfolded, been forced to make crucial changes. Not the least of these was the increasing influence of Red Army commissars – political officers – who had edged in on what Beria had believed was his sole authority to consign dissidents to penal battalions. Sections of the Red Army also resented further incursions by the NKVD.

Victory at Stalingrad would mean far more than military prestige. For Stalin it was a personal mission. For four vital months, during the civil war of 1919–21, the city of Tsaritsyn had been under his personal command. With its name changed to Stalingrad in 1925, it had come to be regarded as a model city, with pleasant open spaces, parks and white apartment blocks. But it was also a key centre for engineering and manufacture, with a university and technical schools. Later it provided supply and storage facilities for the armies on the Don. As the southern bastion of the Soviet Union, it was well defended. Heavy industrial sites in the city included the Tractor Factory (switched to tanks), the Barricades arms plant, the Red October steel works and the Lazur chemical plant.

The Germans intended that Stalingrad should be taken in a three-stage assault by two armies. General Friedrich Paulus's 6th Army would slice through the north, followed by a strike from the south by the 4th Panzer Army of General Hermann Hoth. The final phase would be an assault by Paulus's forces, designed to push any remaining Russian defenders into the Volga. In anticipation of the attack, General Andrei Ivanovich Yeremenko, an unyielding

Ukrainian, was given command of that part of the city running alongside the Tsaritsa River in the city centre.

At dawn on Sunday 23 August 1942, the tanks of Germany's 16th Panzer Division crossed the Don, knifing towards Stalingrad, their crews buoyed with optimism. Above them roared some 600 Junkers and Stukas, carpet-bombing in relays, adding to the heavy damage already inflicted on the city. Colonel General Vasily Chuikov, due to take over command of 62nd Army, later wrote: 'There is not a single green twig on the trees: everything has perished in the flames... All that is left of the wooden houses is a pile of ashes and stove chimneys sticking up out of them.' He described people rummaging desperately amid the ruins, pulling out anything they could salvage.

In Moscow, Stalin was preparing for two separate but interconnected wars. The first was the prosecution of what turned out to be the full savagery of total warfare, the other was a major assault against enemies within, perceived foes of the ideological struggle which had been launched by Lenin.

Prime force

On the field of battle, the prime NKVD force was the 10th NKVD Rifle Division, originating from the Urals and Siberia, consisting of five regiments commanded by Colonel Alexandr Sarayev. The division had made its mark early in July 1941, following the securing of the south-west city of Voronezh, on the Don, which had been threatened by a force of panzer grenadiers. These had been beaten off after ferocious street fighting and heavy losses on each side. At Stalingrad Sarayev's division was given a key role. Its considerable powers included the provision of tank-training and control of river traffic over the Volga.

Sarayev's resources were vital. The speed of the German advance was alarming. The panzers of General Hans Hube's 6th Army made swift progress. They were close to the city's AA guns, whose sound locators had picked up the squeaking treads of the German tanks.

NKVD contingents, together with two tank corps, had dug in around the Stalingrad Tractor Factory, where movement was impeded by blasted streets, bomb craters and ruined buildings.

Fighting gained intensity as, despite the destruction, Hube's tanks ripped through improvised defences and flak guns. By late afternoon, heavy anti-tank fire had slowed down the German armour on the Sukhaya Mechetka Creek, north of the Tractor Factory. After further hours of hard fighting, Hube was forced to withdraw.

However, the Wehrmacht's 16th Panzer Division soon presented a threat to the north of the city, where workers from the industrial suburb of Spartakosvka, under-equipped and badly armed, were drafted into NKVD militia and the notorious destroyer battalions. The main thrust by the Germans was towards the centre in a bid to capture the rail station, then to advance further south, beyond the hill and burial ground of Mamaev Kurgan, also known as Hill 102, which dominated the city. The aim then was to secure the main ferry embankment on the western side of the Volga.

The military value of Sarayev's NKVD forces was doubted within the Red Army. There was a feeling that the division was too weak and widely dispersed to be a wholly effective challenge, particularly as it was also required to maintain order among the civilian population. In aggressive opposition to Sarayev was Commissar Kuzma Akimovich Gurov, who with his egg-bald head, thick eyebrows and bullying demeanour was known to reduce even the mildest critic to a quaking wreck. He waded in with characteristic bluntness, declaring to his chief, Chuikov, head of 62nd Army, to whom Sarayev was also answerable, that 'Sarayev's division was scattered all over the front, and therefore there was practically no control over it. It did not fulfil its function – it hadn't held its defensive positions and it didn't maintain order in the city.'

Glowing report

The NKVD hit back with interest. On 13 October 1942, a glowing report on 10th NKVD Rifle Division was despatched to Beria. The first line read: 'Based in Stalingrad, the 10th Rifle Division played an exceptional role in the defence of the city.' The result was immediate recommendation for the Order of the Red Banner and promotion to the status of a Guards unit, to be followed by the Order of Lenin. In justification for this heaping of honours, achievements were listed as the arrest of 63,547 people, of whom 1,146 were said to be spies, those who had given themselves up or escaped from encirclement.

Criticism of the Red Army was pressed still further. In a report sent to Abakumov, there were complaints of poor combat performance by the Red Army's 92nd Rifle Brigade, which had abandoned a battery of guns it had been unable to shift, implying sheer battlefield incompetence. In self-righteous glee, the NKVD discovered the weapons and lost no time in loading them onto trucks.

Chuikov acted quickly on the doubts that had been cast on the effectiveness of 10th NKVD Rifle Division, seeking meetings with Sarayev, who had been joined by Yeremenko. Chuikov told the pair that he as chief of 62nd Army would be the ultimate boss of all NKVD forces. Their main task was to prepare strongholds within Stalingrad should the Germans break through. Faced with what he regarded as a downgrading of his status, Sarayev clashed bitterly with General Nikolai Krylov, Chuikov's Chief of Staff, but had no alternative but to concur.

Resentment between both sides reached new heights. Chuikov was ruthless and it was the NKVD who were the most proficient at enforcing his orders in and around Stalingrad. Information reached Chuikov that some senior officers had lost heart and had slipped across the Volga in retreat. He decreed that it was NKVD troops who were to control each landing stage and jetty. Another task entrusted to it was to prevent civilians from fleeing. This followed an order from Stalin, who felt that the presence of non-combatants would encourage his troops to fight harder and save the city.

There was a need for Chuikov's strengthened authority. The extent of the damage sustained by the city and the dangers it was facing were dire. Chuikov had some 55,000 men as his sole fighting material, while the Germans had 200,000 troops intent on seizing the city and the main ferry landing points. Mamayev Kurgan changed hands several times. Such locations as the Gorki Theatre and the Univermag department store in Heroes of the Soviet Union Square, defended to the death, became empty shells. Bodies, stinking in the cloying heat, littered the streets.

On 62nd Army's southern base was a giant grain elevator, attacked by 14th and 24th Panzer and 94th Infantry Divisions, preceded by forceful air bombardment and artillery barrages. Hitler, urged on by Goebbels, trumpeted a series of victories. But the truth was that the weary troops of the 6th Army were caught in a battle of attrition.

'Not one step back'

To prevent the Red Army retreating eastwards, Stalin, as People's Commisar for Defence, had, as seen, issued his order 'Not One Step Back', especially designed to inject new urgency into NKVD activity on the front. Specific measures designed to serve the front and immediate operational areas were spelt out in brutal detail. Cowards and those spreading panic were to be 'exterminated on the spot'. All those, including commissars, who withdrew without specific orders were 'betrayers of the Motherland'. Those designated to be guilty of cowardice were to be consigned to the penal battalions, tantamount to a death sentence.

To ram the point home still further, army commanders were ordered to place well-armed blocking detachments of up to 200 men each in the immediate rear of irresolute divisions and require them, in the event of disorderly withdrawal, to execute on the spot cowards and those spreading panic, 'so assisting the divisions' loyal soldiers to discharge their duty to the Motherland'. The blocking detachments were to be provided by 10th NKVD. These troops were formed largely from ordinary military units within the Red Army, which were, however, subject to the orders of the NKVD. They were also responsible for seeking out civilians from recently liberated areas who were the right age for military service.

By early September, 13th Guards Rifle Division, under Stalin's orders, were crossing the Volga in a mix of gunboats, tugs, barges, fishing vessels and rowing boats. Chuikov moved militia battalions under NKVD command to reinforce the Mamayev Kurgan, under threat from the German 100 Jäger Division. On 28 September, the enemy was thrown off its summit. Russian defenders of the grain elevator, which had been assaulted on 18 September, held out for as long as they could, but within days the few survivors had to break out and struggle back to their lines.

When it came to tackling what it perceived to be the enemy within, the NKVD sought to expand its powers. A growing number of reports were sent to Beria and Abakumov and filed by senior personnel who were desperate to make a name for themselves and stress their loyalty. In a report to Beria a Major Selivanovskii stated: 'Recently in connection with the withdrawal of units and formations of the South-Western Front to new lines, a number of anti-Soviet, defeatist and traitorist utterances on the part of several service personnel have been noted.'

The NKVD added almost daily to its roster of offences. These included being in possession of leaflets which the Germans scattered to undermine morale. Anyone found in possession of them, even for the innocent purpose of rolling cigarettes, could be seized. The introduction of strict postal censorship presented opportunities to a vast army of bureaucrats operating under the menacing shadow of Abakumov, head of the Directorate of NKVD Special Section. The section attached to 57th Army (Southern Front) reported that it had dealt with 130,084 items in the postal system. Of these some 7,000 were deemed to contain 'information unsuitable for publication', with others containing 'negative utterances'. Exhaustive investigations were carried out to trace the writers of such traitorous material. The outcome was likely to be arrest and trial before a military tribunal.

Fatigued and disheartened troops received no consideration. A grumbling corporal of 204th Rifle Division was executed for having 'discredited the leaders of the Red Army and uttered terroristic threats against his commanding officer'. There were even cases of thoroughly disgruntled men inventing disloyal remarks by their officers and denouncing them to the NKVD. Many men experienced the sense of being alone and abandoned. They were often bereft of supplies which could only be delivered by dwindling numbers of river craft. Clothing, boots and guns were removed without shame from corpses.

Although the engagement at Stalingrad represented a major triumph for the Red Army, there were, as revealed by Antony Beevor in his detailed account of the battle, incidents of unacceptable behaviour by individual troops which were regarded by their officers as serious breaches of discipline, many of them involving drunkenness. Offenders were hauled before a court presided over by General Vladimir Rogatin, one of the most energetic and ruthless NKVD senior functionaries in charge of front-line discipline. Offenders faced summary firing squads.

There were nonetheless some encouraging moments for 10th NKVD Rifle Division, even if news of them did not always reach the isolated soldiers in the ranks. A report from 271 Regiment revealed that men who had been forced into retreat from the grain elevator area had rallied to launch a counter-attack. By way of encouragement, the division was commended 'for its exemplary execution of combat tasks set by the High Command at the fronts, for its battles with the German invaders, and for the valour and courage manifested therein'.

The honours which had been bestowed on 10th Rifle Division brought little consolation to other troops who could see no end to what was known to the Germans as *Rattenkrieg*, the 'rat war'. Houses and apartment blocks, along with workshops, water towers, railway embankments, walls and cellars formed a cauldron of conflict. Troops from both sides came face to face or jeered and cursed each other across devastated streets. General Hans Doerr of the Wehrmacht later recorded: 'The distance between the enemy's army and ours was as small as it could possibly be. Despite the concentrated activity of aircraft and artillery, it was impossible to break out of the area of close fighting.'

Advent of snipers

With spirits plunging and high casualties among Red Army infantry, the NKVD, fully aware that many of its troops were fighting in the front line and at the behest of Soviet commissars, reconsidered the tactics that were being used. This resulted in the training and deployment of a special sort of combatant. These soldiers were expert at firing from concealed positions over long ranges and were equipped with specially designed or adapted rifles. They were snipers.

Initiatives designed to instil hatred of the Germans were being fed continually to the front lines. It was also made clear to unit heads that they were expected to meet the required quota of potential snipers or they could be consigned to the penal battalions. The intention of the campaign of 'sniperism' was to give the ordinary soldier the chance to make a more tangible contribution to the overall fighting effort.

Throughout training, target competitions were organised. Troops from one division were encouraged to kill more of the enemy than neighbouring divisions. A sniper who achieved forty kills was awarded a 'For Bravery' medal and the titles Noble Sniper and Hero of the Soviet Union. Gradually this policy proved effective. The fame of individual snipers helped to improve morale. But the methods employed bore no relation to previously acceptable rules of warfare; the term 'Noble Sniper' was all too soon an oxymoron. One Soviet sniper, Kovbasa, had no scruples when it came to using fake white flags to deceive Germans, who rose out of their trenches and advanced in the belief that they would become prisoners. Once they were out of cover, Kovbasa lost no time in shooting them down. Snipers operated with marked success from isolated strongholds, which turned out to be highly effective when it came to thwarting the German conquest of Stalingrad. They also played a vital role when they operated with deadly effect from hiding places like chimneys, garrets, cellars and gutted buildings.

Women, many of them already serving in the NKVD as a vital arm of the partisan movement, were by all accounts more than happy to slay their enemies. Typical of these was 19-year-old Tanya Chernova from Belorussia, who willingly exchanged dreams of becoming a ballerina for the zest of front line combat. Following attendance at a sniper school in the Lazar chemical plant between Mamayev Kurgan and the Red October factory, her sole interest became killing as many of the enemy as possible. Individual combatants were merely 'sticks', fit only for breaking. She went on to kill some eighty Germans. Eventually, cut off from a Red Army unit, she and her colleagues, accompanied by a Hiwi (*Hilfsfreiwillige*), a turncoat German volunteer, got lost in a maze of tunnels, emerging from a stinking passage well behind German lines. They concealed their weapons, brazenly joining a queue at a Wehrmacht field kitchen. Fresh from the sewers, though, their pungency attracted attention and they were saved only by the Hiwi, who swiftly claimed that they were working for him. Despite his help, Tanya made no attempt to hide her loathing for him or for any other Hiwis, and wolfed down the bread and soup before escaping. She continued her vendetta against the Germans remorselessly, her career ending abruptly when a fellow sniper, whom she denounced in fury as 'a stupid cow', trod on a mine, resulting in serious injuries for both of them. Tanya had to be evacuated across the Volga and out of the war.

The importance of women snipers for the war effort resulted in the creation of the Central Women's School for Sniper Training near Moscow, headed by N.P. Chegodaeva, who was a veteran of the Spanish Civil War. The school turned out more than 1,000 women snipers and 407 instructors, who proved the value of their training by, it was later claimed, killing around 12,000 German soldiers.

Snipers frequently worked in pairs. In a celebrated action, one couple elected to die simultaneously. Mariya Polivanova and Natalaya Kovshovaya had killed more than 300 Germans before they were pinned in near Novgorod on 14 August 1942, to the south of Leningrad. They went on firing until there was no ammunition left, save for the two grenades they were clutching. They waited for the Germans to advance, then blew themselves up, taking some of the enemy with them. Their ultimate honour was to be made Heroes of the Soviet Union. In all ninety-two women were awarded this honour during the war.

Along with their involvement in helping to develop a body of effective snipers, the NKVD had other preoccupations. Not the least of these was what was regarded as the arrogant behaviour of the commissars when working with senior members of the army. This attitude was profoundly resented within the ranks. Sensitive to the dangers of this tension when it was essential that the army should have strong morale, Stalin, on 9 October 1942, let it be known that the role of the commissars would be downgraded. The NKVD was detailed to take notes of soldiers' reactions. Most were favourable. One officer was quoted as declaring: 'All military men support this decision. There must be only one chain of command within the army.' Generally, there was a widespread feeling that the presence of commissars at Stalingrad was irrelevant, particularly as some of them possessed little military training.

However, none of these measures relieved the horrors within the city, where in the graphic phrase of a German officer 'the street is no longer measured in metres but in corpses'. To all outward appearances Paulus still held the advantage. On 4 October, he launched an assault on the three remaining Soviet strong-points: the Tractor Factory, the Barricades arms plant and the Red October steel works. Within a month, the Germans had reduced the Russian-held area to two small enclaves. But in no way could Hitler match the level of Soviet reinforcements – some 132,500 heavy guns, 900 tanks and 11,000 aircraft – being marshalled by Zhukov. During this crucial phase of the battle, Paulus's best troops were hemmed in at Stalingrad itself, while the rest of the extended front was held by Romanians, Hungarians and Italians, who were for the most part poorly equipped, notably with obsolete anti-tank guns.

Operation Uranus

On 18 November, Chuikov received a call from front headquarters, alerting him and his men to Operation Uranus, designed to cut off the Germans with a massive counter-offensive launched from neighbouring fronts. The plan involved the destruction of the German-Romanian forces operating in the Don bend and in the vicinity of Stalingrad.

Zhukov, among others, had managed to win over Stalin when it came to appointing the right commanders for mechanised warfare, irrespective of past enmities. An outstanding example was General Konstantin Rokossovsky, who during the Civil War had fought with distinction against the White Guard armies and received the Order of the Red Banner. This counted for nothing at the time of the Great Purge, when he was arrested by the NKVD, which accused him of 'connections with foreign intelligence'.

He had fallen out with many of the traditionalists within the old guard commanders, who had favoured cavalry tactics rather than the creation of a strong armoured corps for the Red Army. It proved a handy pretext for Beria to move in. His interrogation included torture, which resulted in the loss of nine teeth, three cracked ribs, the removal of his finger nails. He was subjected to mock firing squads. But now Rokossovsky became commander of the Don front, stretching from the northern tip of Stalingrad westwards to Kletskaya, just beyond the great Don bend.

The first blow was an attack against the northern flank of Army Group B on the Don, followed by a second blow directed at the southern flank on the Kalmyk steppe which bordered on the western shore of the Caspian Sea. These positions were defended by the Romanians; all disintegrated in chaos.

Bitter fighting broke out on all sides. For example, on 11 November Colonel Ivan Lyudnikov's 138th Division advanced on a narrow strip of land which was held by Germans bereft of sufficient food and ammunition. Nevertheless their resistance was fierce, and Lyudnikov's forces were bombed in relays by the Luftwaffe, which scattered leaflets, urging surrender. Two days later there was hand-to-hand fighting. Now it was the turn of Lyudnikov's men to suffer from inadequate supplies and they were forced to use ammunition captured from the Germans. On the orders of Lyudnikov, NKVD blocking detachments and security staff were mustered for the front line. He also made use of mobile combat formations because they could provide all-round fire when encountering the enemy in heavily defended buildings.

By the closing days of November, both pincers of the Soviet offensive closed behind the German positions. 6th Army was trapped. Twenty German and two Romanian divisions were cut off at Stalingrad. Threatened German troops in the Caucasus and the Don were edging away. In the same month, Hitler recalled Feldmarschall Erich von Manstein from the Leningrad front and put him in charge of a newly-created formation. This was Army Group Don, made up of Paulus's 6th Army, the remnants of the severely mauled Romanian armies and Hoth's panzer army. The overall aim was to push through from the south-west and relieve 6th Army. Hoth's panzers were to carve a corridor through the Russian lines in order to present Paulus with a chance to break out.

But Paulus refused to move without Hitler's consent. Hoth's forces were fought to a standstill and eventually Manstein ordered him to withdraw.

Target collaborators

During the course of Operation Uranus, NKVD units followed in the wake of the Red Army, passing through villages that had been in German hands. Their targets were collaborators, particularly those who had denounced their fellow inhabitants to the Feldpolizei, and deserters. The Soviet forces had suffered from a high incidence of desertion. Deserters were be either shot in front of a couple of hundred of their fellows, or, more usually, led off behind the lines by a squad from an NKVD guard detachment. At a convenient spot they were ordered to strip for the purely practical reason that their uniform and boots could be passed to others. At Stalingrad, the NKVD executed around 13,500 Soviet troops, the equivalent of an entire division.

The ultimate effect of such bloodletting was widely deplored. Critics of the NKVD claimed that it was over-concerned with enforcing the harshest discipline within the Red Army, rather than coming up with valuable intelligence. Empire-building was also rife within the organisation, especially within the squads of the special detachments whose agents were reckoned to have executed thousands of troops for instances of vaguely defined 'defeatism'. Failure to apprehend and despatch prisoners was condemned as 'sentimentality'.

Released NKVD documents report the allegedly verbatim confessions of so-called 'cowards and panic mongers', but historians regard these with some caution, suggesting that many may well have been prepared in advance for signature by those accused, who would have been threatened with torture. In an instance of damning self-indictment a junior political instructor, whose name survives solely as Shilkin, officially stated:

> I confess that I deserted the battlefield, leaving the soldiers on the defence line. I deserted because I lacked confidence in the strength of the soldiers' resistance in my platoon. It seemed to

me that they would not stand up to the pressure of the Germans and would run away. But it turned out differently. The soldiers stood their ground and I behaved like a coward and ran away.

According to the report, Shilkin was shot in front of his unit.

In addition, during the course of the NKVD investigations, another victim, battalion commissar Lukin, acknowledged his guilt. 'In the intense fighting I did not take the necessary decisive steps towards those soldiers who arbitrarily abandoned the brigade without any order from the army's command.' Lukin, too, was shot.

Within Stalingrad itself, the Russians hung on, and the grip of the NKVD remained firm on the Volga. On New Year's Eve, the Volga had locked solid with ice. Supply trucks were able to cross with food and ammunition. The mood had lightened and it proved infectious. There was even a New Year's Eve party with actors and musicians sent in by high-ranking Soviet officers to entertain the troops. But always there was the grim presence of the NKVD, standing between the front line and the Volga, checking soldiers' papers and shooting suspected deserters. Red Army troops crossing the Volga faced a solid wall of flame, while the NKVD guards fired at the deserters who attempted to run away after landing.

Paulus's plight was steadily worsening. He was soon radioing that he possessed only seventy tons of supplies and could hold out no longer than a matter of days. On the Russian side, men and resources were under great strain. Since there was no chance that the German 6th Army could continue to resist, the Russians presented an ultimatum for surrender. Under a flag of truce, two envoys, Captain Nikolay Dmitrevich Dyatlenko of the NKVD, a German speaker, and Major Aleksandr Mikhailovich Smyslov of army intelligence were chosen to deliver the terms. Their mission, however, failed; the Germans refused to contemplate a ceasefire and the two men returned to their posts unharmed.

On 8 January 1943, Rokossovky urged the Germans to surrender. Paulus signalled Hitler, asking for 'freedom of action' and received the reply: 'Capitulation is impossible. The Sixth Army will do its historic duty at Stalingrad until the last man, in order to make possible the reconstruction of the western front.' On 30 January, Paulus radioed Hitler: 'Final collapse cannot be delayed more than 24 hours.' In his last headquarters in the south of the city, in the face of defeat, he proclaimed his loyalty to the last. 'The swastika flag is still flying high over Stalingrad. May our battle be an example to the present and coming generations...'

In order to stiffen Paulus's resolve, Hitler promoted him to field marshal, proclaiming that never had a German field marshal surrendered. Promotion grades were also bestowed on 115 other officers. Paulus took refuge on a camp bed within his final headquarters, too demoralised for active command. On 31 January, he stepped out from the darkened cellar of his headquarters and made his own personal surrender to the Soviet commander of 64th Army, to be followed two days later by troops holding out in the north.

The end of the bulk of fighting within Stalingrad led to the massive dispersal of prisoners. That meant an increased role for the NKVD's Main Directorate for POW and Internees (GUPVI), which had been established in September 1939 following the Soviet invasion of Poland. Its chief was Lieutenant General Ivan Petrov, a trusted colleague of Beria who had worked with the NKVD blocking forces in the Caucasian passes. Bleakly factual reports of the fate of prisoners over wide areas flooded Petrov's desk. Of the 91,000 Germans who surrendered at Stalingrad, 27,000 died within weeks, although Paulus's army was starved and frostbitten when captured, and only five per cent, mainly officers, survived. GUPVI operated in parallel with the similar GULAG system. As in the GULAG, prisoners faced hard labour, poor nutrition and living conditions and a high rate of mortality.

Those who deserted to the Germans at a time when victory over Russia had seemed likely were other targets of the NKVD. Singled out were men who joined German regiments and wore German uniforms. Initially, Hitler had banned their recruitment, regarding them as sub-human (*Untermensch*) Slavs of no value to the 'Aryan' German army. However, as his fortunes declined, their manpower became essential; at one time these men came to represent over a quarter of the strength of 6th Army frontline divisions, put at some

50,000. Within their ranks there was a strict hierarchy with three distinct groups. First were troops, so-called Cossack sections, who had been mobilised by the Germans and attached to divisions; then came voluntary assistants, deserters and volunteers who deserted to join the Germans, while those in the third category were regarded with something approaching contempt: they did the so-called 'dirty jobs' in kitchens and stables. In the words of one captured Hiwi: 'The categories are treated differently, volunteers treated best.'

Additionally, many Russians being held in German prison camps had been persuaded by the Germans to volunteer in the hope that they would eventually be returned home. They were soon disillusioned and were thrust into the front line. Those who fell into the hands of the Red Army were dubbed 'former Russians' and were invariably executed for their treason by NKVD firing squads.

Stalin's reaction to revelations about the number of Soviet turncoats who had served the Germans only fuelled his obsession for hunting out traitors and collaborators. He focused on the success of the man who was to become one of the Second World War's master spies. This was Reinhardt Gehlen, who had been working extensively on the eastern front, had been promoted to senior intelligence officer and had achieved some notable successes by infiltrating agents behind Soviet lines. At a meeting of senior colleagues in April 1943, Stalin called for the creation of a special department to tackle the scourge presented by Gehlen.

Chapter 6

Enter SMERSH

Although it has been ruthlessly exploited by writers of spy fiction, SMERSH, the new security department that was created at this time, had a very real existence. At first it was suggested that it should be titled SMERNESH (*Smert nemetskim shpionam*, death to German spies). According to some Soviet accounts, Stalin asked: 'And why as a matter of fact should we be speaking only of German spies? Aren't other intelligence services working against our country? Let's call it *Smert Shpionam*'. What emerged was SMERSH, acronym for 'Death to spies'.

SMERSH was to become a leviathan, growing out of the existing Directorate of Special Operations whose umbrella was the NKVD. Officially, SMERSH was entirely separate from the NKVD and the other security organ, the NKGB, whose speciality was police and counter-intelligence. But the truth was that the three frequently worked together, shaping an organisation which in four short years killed thousands of men and women, leaving behind a legacy of terror unequalled even in the annals of the Chekists.

Although, as was to be expected, Beria was keen to establish an ongoing role for the NKVD, his authority was now lessened: he was obliged to take orders from the Council of Ministers, the Soviet Union's highest executive and administrative body. Frictions were inevitable, caused particularly by Stalin, who insisted on his own sources for information. Directly answerable to him was Viktor Abakumov, Beria's old rival, now put in charge of military counter-intelligence, with full powers of arrest.

A single directorate of SMERSH became responsible for the surveillance of staff officers assigned to the Moscow-based Soviet General Staff headquarters. They were by no means the only soldiers to be spied on. Individual members of troop units stationed in and around Moscow gained the attentions of SMERSH. One of the main areas of concern was the threat that could be posed by any semblance of rebellion within the armed forces. SMERSH went ahead to create some two million spies working within the forces, although post-war sources have put the figure as high as 3,400,000.

Tagged as 'Top Secret of Special Importance' and issued on 21 April 1943 with the authority of Stalin as Chairman of the State Defence Committee was the organisation's statute. This was couched in such terms as to make the powers and authority of SMERSH agencies in the field of defence abundantly clear.

> Operational, counter-espionage and other measures were to be taken in order to create conditions at the fronts eliminating the possibilities of enemy agents passing through the front line with impunity. And to make the front line impassable for spies and anti-Soviet elements.

There were seven administrative departments, two of which were responsible for collating information and dropping agents behind enemy lines. Measures to extend the work of the NKVD way beyond Soviet frontiers were nothing new. Back in October 1940 Order No. 00648 had created yet another entry in the alphabet soup of acronyms. This one had been SHON, standing for *Shkola Osobogo Naznacheniya*, Special Purpose School, a bland title for a top-notch training academy in foreign intelligence, drawing its recruits for the most part from the cream of academia within Moscow, Leningrad, Kiev and beyond. Demands on them were considerable, not least scrupulous security screening for each entrant.

The workload, by any standards, was gruelling. Tuition in foreign languages took up four hours a day, followed by two hours on the trade craft of intelligence. In complete contrast to previous communist orthodoxy were courses on the social, economic and cultural backgrounds of western countries, seen as indispensable for those likely to be infiltrated. Germany, naturally enough, was the obvious target. Hand-picked and few in number, these agents succeeded in penetrating the country's intelligence schools and camps, bringing back valuable information.

For example, a report to the State Defence Committee, dated 22 July 1943, cited the exploits of an agent code-named 'Severov', who reported back to his superiors details of ninety-three German intelligence officers and 133 agents intended for deployment behind enemy lines. A useful bonus was photographs of German intelligence officers and agents.

When it came to establishing an effective espionage arm, the NKVD, when operating on its own, had been a mere minnow, plagued by weakened military leadership and Stalin's obsession with purges. It had been regarded as a fledging organisation, seen by many as ineffective in the face of Hitler's startling rise to power. By the time of Barbarossa, however, it had been able to build up a Europe-wide network of communist sympathisers and activists. Concentration was focused on the premier training schools for agents of the German Abwehr. One of these schools, at Sulejowek, a small town near Warsaw, was penetrated by a Lieutenant Voinov, who, posing as a German instructor, was able to send home the names and photographs of German agents, together with codes and deployment schedules, resulting in the arrest of more than 100 of them.

'Red Orchestra'

One of the most remarkable operations was in the hands of two resistance groups, jointly codenamed *die Rote Kapelle*, the 'Red Orchestra', so called because the Abwehr's Nazi-speak dubbed Soviet spies' radio transmitters as 'music boxes' and their operators as 'musicians'.

NKVD talent spotters went on to muster one of its shrewdest and most ruthless operators. Codenamed Gilbert, Leopold Trepper, born in 1904, had been steeped in revolution right from his teenage days as an impoverished Polish Jewish shop-keeper's son. He was forced to abandon his studies at Kracow university and become a communist aged 21. He had not been solely driven by ideology; he also needed a job. He was given a probationary post within the State Police Administration of the GPU, the political directorate which had grown out of the Cheka. Calculated networking had saved him from elimination in the purges. He was eventually groomed by his

Soviet spymasters to be the agent responsible for their western European circuit: grand chef of the spy cadre of Rote Kapelle.

Trepper, who was answerable to Soviet military counter-intelligence, was given the task of building up a circuit in Belgium run by Johann Wenzel (codenamed Hermann and widely known as 'the Professor'). This led to a contact with a group in Berlin established by Harro (codename Starshina) and his wife Libertas Schulze-Boysen. Harro's work in air intelligence, including at one point transfer to the attaché group, had made him invaluable to the Soviets. He gained access to target maps of the Luftwaffe bomber force and to a spread of reports from German air attachés worldwide. Of even greater value were drawings of the latest Luftwaffe equipment, arms production and precise routes of Allied convoys. He worked with another couple, Arvid and Mildred Harnack, the former a seemingly incorruptible civil servant and National Socialist Party member. Harnack was in fact a devoted communist who had been recruited as an agent in 1933.

The organisation which Trepper went on to mastermind was a highly impressive espionage network embedded within the Third Reich and eventually the countries which it overran. Ultimately responsible to the NKVD was Trepper's control, codenamed Erdburg, whose intention was to combine the Harnack spy network with that of Schulze-Boysen's.

With the unleashing of Barbarossa, swift contact was made with the senior agents in Germany, who were forbidden to assemble in one place where they could be easily rounded up. They received their instructions in subway stations and at tram stops where Erdburg handed over suitcases.

Soon Moscow agents were able to study a cluster of flags on their situation maps, each of which denoted a Rote Kapelle cell. It emerged that one of the most effective was in Brussels, the centre of a network spawning Soviet informers and agents all over Germany. Military and industrial intelligence in occupied Europe was scooped into the net, along with data on troop deployments, availability of raw material, aircraft production and tank designs.

Everything looked set for success – until a radio operator on dawn shifts at the Kranz monitoring station in East Prussia was instructed to track the output of a small transmitter tucked away in the mountains and operated by Norwegian partisans. The terrain had long acted as a screen and made the signals hard to pinpoint. Then, without warning, had come an unusual call sign: '*KLK from PTX... KLK from PTX... KLK from PTX... AR 50383 KLX from PTK*'.

The ensuing message consisted of cypher groups. The operator reported his new discovery, listing the frequency. The Reich's most highly-qualified radio operators working in counter-espionage wrestled to decode it. Within hours of it being received, teleprinters rattled out an order to all Wehrmacht direction-finding stations, which eventually discovered that call sign PTX was beamed straight to Moscow. Its origin was eventually narrowed to the Etterbeek quarter of Brussels and in particular three houses in the Rue des Atrebes, used by Trepper's agents. In the fireplace of No.101, Gestapo operatives found a fragment of an encoded message. Their questioning of the housekeeper worked wonders.

Transmissions to Moscow were severed. Soon it became clear that Gestapo and Abwehr investigations were getting dangerously close to the cell in Berlin. To make matters worse, the NKVD had been guilty of a monumental blunder when a message from it had been accompanied by the addresses of promising new agents.

Fearful that the Gestapo would arrest him, Schulze-Boysen made a warning telephone call to a close associate, Corporal Horst Heilmann from the Luftwaffe Signals Services, whom he had recruited. But Heilmann had been unable to take the call. Schulze-Boysen made the fatal mistake of leaving his name, which soon reached the Gestapo. It was all the Germans needed. Black limousines sped through dawn streets. Schulze-Boysen and his wife Libertas were among the first to be thrown into the cellars of the Prinz Albrechtstrasse jail, along with the Harnacks, who were picked up holidaying in East Prussia. A further blow came with the capture in Belgium of Johann Wenzel, the Professor, the hitherto invaluable contact with Dutch and French communists whom he had trained in radio. On 16 November 1942, Trepper himself was captured from a dentist's chair, where he found himself staring down the barrels of two revolvers. Soon the arrests had become so numerous that a Rote Kapelle special section had to be created.

The success of the mop-up in the Rue des Atrebus proved especially galling. One of the Rote Kapelle leaders there was Abraham Raichman, a Polish-Jewish forger, specialising in passports and rubber stamps. Indifferent to politics and happy to forge for anyone who shared his passion, Raichman needed no persuasion to change sides and work for the Germans.

In Switzerland, Dr Otto Punter (codename Pakbo), organiser and cryptographer of the Soviet espionage circuit, flashed an encoded message to Soviet headquarters:

> To Director. Through Pakbo. A large-scale organisation providing information to the Soviet Union was discovered in Berlin in September. Many arrests have been made and more are imminent. The Gestapo hopes to be able to uncover the entire organisation.

In the hope that Trepper might also be persuaded to cross to the Germans, the Gestapo kept him on ice. In the guise of feeding disinformation to Moscow, he managed to insert some coded hints that he had been captured. Of the Schulze-Boysen/Harnack groups, on 22 December 1942 the men had been executed in Plotzensee prison by slow strangulation, on orders confirmed by Hitler. The women had been guillotined. The Trepper ring had been eliminated.

At the war's end and with his return to Russia, Trepper's reception was predictable and mirrored by thousands. Instead of greeting him as a hero, Stalin was convinced he was a traitor and had him flung into the Lubyanka. There were those who maintained that Trepper had simply become a victim of Stalin's countless anti-Jewish pogroms, while others suspected that the Nazis had succeeded in convincing Moscow that Leopold Trepper had been working for Germany all along and had deliberately betrayed his own agents. His fate was to be subjected to hours of grilling by Abakumov, surviving in the prison's harshest conditions until eventual release under the rule of Khrushchev.

On the battle fronts SMERSH's main activity was rooting out spies. Their methods were characterised by swift brutality. An instance was witnessed by Lev Mistetskiy, a Kiev-born Jew, a field engineer advancing with his battalion on the town of Kamenets-Podolskiy in the western Ukraine:

> Two soldiers joined us. They wore ordinary uniforms. We asked them who they were, and they replied they had escaped from captivity and wanted to join a military unit. Our commanding officer unbuttoned the shirt on one of them: there was German underwear underneath. He shot both of them. There were SMERSH officers in each regiment. Their task was to identify spies at the front line, but most of the time they investigated what the military talked about and whether some of them weren't happy about the situation. They treated those as they had treated enemies of the people before the war. At the beginning of the war our army incurred big losses and many military were captured. If some of them managed to escape they were subject to investigation by SMERSH officers. Very often those people who had taken every effort to escape and get to their own forces were arrested and exiled... In most cases these were innocent people, but SMERSH officers just needed grounds to arrest people and they usually got them. They had their informers in each unit and you could never be sure that you weren't talking to an informer.

SMERSH agents were kept busy trawling correspondence in search of what was regarded as heretical comment. In one instance, a lieutenant who in a letter had been unwise enough to praise the expertise of Luftwaffe pilots, and the inability of his own forces to shoot down sufficient enemy aircraft, was condemned as a traitor. Families of those captured by the enemy, even if totally innocent, were not immune from punishment. A considerable coup for the Germans was securing incriminating documents which had been in the hands of a senior NKVD officer, a member of the Supreme Soviet responsible for the fortifications of Leningrad. The man's three sisters, all of whom worked for the NKVD, were swiftly dismissed. Two were thrown out of their apartments, the other was exiled.

Dissident groups were especially vulnerable and were likely to be infiltrated by SMERSH agents who, posing as supporters, were required to recruit around eight likely informers, each of whom was given a codename. These were required to sign a secrecy pledge and to report any detected instances of anti-Soviet activity to their personal recruiter. The effect was to supply SMERSH with a steady stream of informers. There was to be no freedom for them even when their reports were completed: their personal files remained in the hands of the NKVD.

When it came to ensuring security in captured territories, responsibility lay with the NKVD, which was in charge of the vast network of frontier guard posts and check points. Every citizen contacted in the area was required by law to report treason or 'counter revolutionary crimes' or face six months to ten years of imprisonment. Individuals who were reluctant to concur tended to give way in the face of threats to their families. In addition, units patrolled cities and villages, tasked with combating any semblance of anti-Soviet behaviour.

There were no exceptions when it came to recruiting likely talent for front line conflict, including teenagers from the Young Pioneers, part of the Communist Party's overall programme to inculcate party ideology into children and young adults aged between fourteen and twenty-seven years of age, a movement branded the Komosol. Those deemed promising material were forged and tempered for war. One of the Komosol's toughest training schools was at Kuchino, near Moscow. Lessons in unarmed combat and proficiency in the use of weapons were provided, and a laboratory carried out continuous production of effective narcotics and poisons.

New weapons were constantly devised. Nikolai Evgenievich Khokhlov, a former officer of the NKVD and SMERSH, was one of the first high-ranking Soviet intelligence agents to defect to the west after the war. He brought with him a 'cigarette-case' which fired dum-dum bullets through the tips of cigarettes, and an electrically fired revolver so small that it could be concealed in the palm of a hand and when fired was virtually inaudible. Another defector, Bogdan Stashynsky, trained in an assassination school in Minsk and given the codename Oleg, gave himself up to US officials in Berlin, revealing details of another weapon:

...a metal tube about as thick as a finger and about seven

inches long, and consisting of three sections screwed together. In the bottom section there is a firing-pin which is fixed and can be released by pressing a spring that can be bolted; the firing pin then ignites a powder charge (a small percussion cap). This causes a metal lever in the middle section to move; it crushes a glass ampoule in the orifice of the tube. This glass ampoule, with a volume of five cubic centimetres... contains a poison that in appearance resembles water and escapes out of the front of the tube in the form of vapour when the ampoule is crushed. If this vapour is fired at a person's face from a distance of about one and a half feet, the person drops dead immediately upon inhaling the vapour... Since this vapour leaves no traces, it is impossible to ascertain death by violence, and... the perpetrator suffers no harmful effects from the poison if he swallows a certain kind of tablet beforehand as an antidote and immediately after firing the weapon, crushes an ampoule sewn up in gauze and inhales the vapour.

Throughout its turbulent existence, SMERSH appropriated many of the practices of the NKVD, not least its routine brutality. In the course of a BBC radio interview in 1999 Zinaida Pytkina, a former woman officer in SMERSH, related how she shot a young German major after his interrogation. A grave had been dug and the officer was made to kneel down. Pytkina had then drawn her pistol and fired. 'My hand didn't tremble. It was a joy for me... The Germans didn't ask us to spare them and I was angry... I fulfilled my task. And I went back to the office.'

Uneasy rivalry

The NKVD had stepped up the hunt for German agents particularly active as spies and saboteurs. Within the Reich, preparing these agents had been the responsibility of the Abwehr, with whom the NKVD had frequently worked in uneasy rivalry until the advent of Barbarossa. From then on, the priority of the two organisations was to outsmart each other. A typical example of this rivalry came on 22 April 1942. The NKVD, as part of a countrywide sweep codenamed Operation Quartz, attached its 5th Rifle Division to the Leningrad area of Tikhivin. They had seized a German spy wearing the uniform of a Red Army junior lieutenant named Ivan Golovanov. He and others captured would have been shot out of hand if they had been apprehended by the Red Army. Instead, the NKVD turned them into double agents. They became involved with the Germans in *Funkspiele*, 'radio games', with the purpose of entrapping still more agents. Their antics became surreal when it emerged that the Germans were doing precisely the same thing.

A notable coup for the Soviets was a German agent codenamed Malakhov who was captured with his hand-held radio set. After unscrambling his codes, contact was made with the Germans and Malakov was persuaded to ask for new batteries for his set. Matters then passed into the capable hands of Lieutenant Yevgeniy Serebrov of the NKVD's counter-espionage department. The Germans were informed that Malakov would be able to organise the theft of apparently key documents from one of the Soviet military commands. The aim was to entice German agents who would also be 'turned', if necessary after being drawn into a 'honey trap' with a personable female agent.

On a broader front, Hitler was conscious of the appalling effect of the German defeat at Stalingrad on both civil and military morale within Germany and the danger of possible rebellion in restless occupied countries. He realised that any inaction could provide a potentially fatal advantage to the Russians.

He decided to take the offensive in central Russia. He chose an area south of Orel and north of Belgorod and Kharkov. Here a Soviet salient 160 miles across jutted into the German front line. Nazi intelligence had revealed vast offensive Soviet strength at this point, backed by massive reserves. After delays caused by the build-up of German forces, the operation, codenamed *Zitadelle* (Citadel), was launched on 5 July 1943.

As it turned out, the first strike of the offensive at 2.30am was not German, but a powerful amalgam of heavy artillery and scores of multi-barrelled Katyusha rockets from secure positions behind the Russian front line. It was a pre-emptive strike conceived by Red Army senior commanders after intelligence had been received from Switzerland-based Rudolf Rossler, a small, bespectacled middle-class German émigré, publisher and liberal, codenamed Lucy. He had been paid by the NKGB to pass details to Moscow of German political and military developments, including copies of plans for Barbarossa. His contacts included a circle of anti-Nazis working in OKW (*Oberkommando der Wehrmacht*, the German High Command), the most senior of whom was believed to be Major General Hans Oster, chief of staff to the head of the Abwehr, Admiral Wilhelm Canaris. It was considered likely that Lucy passed critical information to Stalin, giving Hitler's instructions for the *Zitadelle* attack.

Switzerland was not the only conduit for anti-Nazi intelligence. Specialists at the British cipher and code centre at Bletchley Park, a country house fifty miles north-west of London, had the task of decoding highly complex messages from Germany's top-secret cypher machine (*Schusselmaschine E* – Enigma). The most sensitive information decoded was given the codename 'Ultra', some of it deemed so secret that even the Russians received only specially filtered data. Nevertheless, a great deal of secret information did reach Moscow by other routes.

'Cambridge Five'

Moscow's informant was Anatoli Gromov, a wily energetic NKVD recruiter who had held the post of London resident since November 1940 with cover posts of attaché, then second secretary of the Soviet Embassy. His responsibilities included the control of eighteen agents, including the so-called 'Cambridge Five', members of a Soviet spy ring in the United Kingdom who had become committed communists during or after attending Cambridge University in the 1930s. The ring included Kim Philby (codenamed Stanley), Donald Maclean (Homer), Guy Burgess (Hicks), Anthony Blunt (Johnson) and John Cairncross (Henry), later identified as 'the fifth man'. Since Cairncross worked at Bletchley Park, he was of particular interest to Anatoli Gromov, who recruited him. With money supplied by the NKVD, Cairncross was bought a car, which on his days off he drove to London with Ultra material.

Hitler remained set on *Zitadelle*, not least because of a deep-seated fear that if the Russians succeeded in slicing their way through the salient they would have a clear route to the Ukraine. He was in favour of encircling the enemy with a powerful punch from two attacking armies. But there were dissenting voices protesting that an Allied landing in Italy was expected, which would mean switching available forces to the Mediterranean. Furthermore, German resources were already stretched, which had caused Hitler to postpone the launch of the operation three times.

However, on 1 July he told an assembly of senior commanders that he intended *Zitadelle* to start within five days. Previous delays and the final short notice were to prove fatal miscalculations. By the time that General Walther Model's 9th Army in the north and Generaloberst Hans Hoth's 4th Panzer Army in the south were able to roll, Hitler's procrastination had worked in his enemy's favour. Due to the timely data received from Lucy, Soviet bombers made a number of pre-emptive strikes on seventeen German airfields which Cairncross had been able to pinpoint in his reports. It was later reckoned that, out of 1,400 flown sorties, more than 500 Luftwaffe aircraft were destroyed on the ground. Of even of greater value was the fact that the NKVD was furnished with a series of Enigma intercepts, identifying the positions not only of individual aircraft, but of entire Luftwaffe squadrons.

In addition, the Russians had built up an immense programme of defensive works, including belts of minefields and a network of highly effective anti-tank strongholds, vital in what was to be a battle of tanks. For Russian success in this tank war, the NKVD's contribution via Cairncross was invaluable. Attention focused on the armour of the 60-ton PzKW VI Tiger 1, which had been in production since the previous August. The Germans believed that Soviet cannon would be unable to penetrate the Tigers' thick armour, a claim which reached Ultra intelligence. In consequence, Soviet engineers were spurred to design and subsequently manufacture appropriate armour-piercing shells. It was also learnt that a main weakness of the Tigers was that they required intensive maintenance and were prone to mechanical failures if periodic procedures were not carried out. These factors, combined with heavy weight, contributed to low operational mobility. During retreats these problems were particularly serious because damaged Tigers could not be reovered and had to be destroyed by their crews.

When it came to the day of the battle on Monday 5 July, unspeakable weather turned the battlefield, notably in the north, into a quagmire. The tactical rule book – that the purpose of the panzers was to exploit enemy weakness rather than pitch tank against tank – was blown into oblivion. One of the worst areas of slaughter, lying to the north-east of Belgorod, was Prokhorovka. Here during the climax of the battle it was difficult to see the land and the sky – a yawning nothingness was created by clouds of dust and smoke. The Russian tanks, the T34s and heavy KVs (Klimont Voroshilovs), struck across the flank of the Tigers and Panthers, the latter considered by many to be by far the best German tanks of the war. Drivers and commanders could not see where they were going, tanks smashed into each other and were destroyed by their own side, and the steppe was littered with wreckage. Oil and blood from both sides stained the silver-grey grass. The sky was black from the smoke of the fires.

Hitler summoned von Manstein, who had command of the armies of Generals Model and Hoth, along with Feldmarschall Gunther von Kluge, commanding Army Group Centre, to his East Prussian headquarters, where he announced that he was calling off *Zitadelle*.

In Moscow the mood was ecstatic, strikingly caught by one of many newspaper headlines: 'THE TIGERS ARE BURNING'. The last major German offensive in Russia had failed. Hot on the heels of the Red Army's triumph, the NKVD searched out the areas laid waste by the battle, looking for the inevitable deserters, many of whom discarded their uniforms in the hope of being taken for civilians.

The Soviet Supreme High Command had by this time ordered the creation of an independent army of NKVD troops, comprising six divisions. This formation, designated 70th Army, had been deployed on the central front and had gone on to fight at Kursk. The ruthless methods used to subjugate not only its own forces, but also ordinary Soviet civilians, were observed by German soldiers. A good example of this is the method used by the 70th Army to create lanes through uncharted minefields, designed to ease the advance of the armoured regiments. In a letter home, a Wehrmacht soldier wrote:

> One feature of Soviet attacks was the numbers involved. One day, during the retreat [from Kursk] we found out how these were obtained. Apparently as we withdraw, the Red Army reoccupies the area and rounds up all adult civilians, men and women alike. These are formed into makeshift workers' battalions and then sent into attacks to make up weight and numbers. It does not matter that these conscripts are untrained, that many are without boots of any kind, and that most of them have no weapons. Prisoners whom we took told us that those without weapons are expected to take up those from the fallen. These unarmed civilians forced to accompany the assault had been suspected of collaboration with us and were paying, in many cases quite literally, with their lives because of this suspicion.
>
> I saw other attacks which were preceded by solid blocks of people marching shoulder to shoulder across the minefields which we had laid. Civilians and army punishment battalions alike advanced like automata, their ranks broken only wherein a mine exploded, killing and wounding those around it. The people seemed never to flinch nor to quail and we noticed that some who fell were then shot by a smaller wave of commissars or officers who followed very closely behind the blocks of punishment victims. What these people had done to deserve this sort of treatment is unknown, but we found among prisoners whom we took, officers who had failed to gain a given objective, NCOs who had lost a machine-gun in action and men whose crime had been to fall out of the line of march. These stragglers, swept up by flying columns, were given a hasty court-martial and then sentenced to unbelievably long terms of imprisonment. Some of them had to serve part of their sentence clearing mines and in these cases this was carried out by blocks of men tramping forward across our gardens of death.
>
> And yet none, or very few, ever complained at their

treatment. Life was hard, they said, and if you failed to achieve a target you paid for your failure. A given task had to be accomplished or dire punishment was the expected and the accepted result.

Both Ultra and Lucy revealed that Hitler could expect no further reinforcements; troops in western Europe, facing the prospect of Allied invasion, could not be spared, while on the Eastern Front the German armies had few reserves. But all this did not mean the final immolation of Hitler's forces.

The Führer's attention now focused on Kharkov, the Soviet Union's fourth most important city, lying about 300 miles east of Kiev, which he declared must be held whatever the cost. The city had already changed hands several times. The victory by the German 6th Army on 24 October 1941 had met with little resistance, but it had been a deep source of wounded pride to Russians when, in a bid to recapture it with 640,000 troops and 1,200 tanks, two German armies had seen them off. Matters had been reversed after Soviet troops made a breakout from Stalingrad in February 1943 and retook the city, only to see it recaptured the following month by the German Army Group South. Here was a city of shattered buildings, craters of rubble, and surviving inhabitants who were living without power and water. But not for the first or last time, Stalin treated forces at Kharkov as objects of suspicion, convincing himself that, since they had failed on two occasions to hold the city, there must have been traitors within their ranks who had rendered aid to German occupation forces.

Retribution was assigned to the NKVD. Generaloberst Erhard Raus, commander of the newly formed XI Corps of General Army Detachment (*Armeeabteilung*) Kempf, later wrote:

> Entering Zolochev, a small city 20 miles north of Kharkov, our troops had occasion to discover the extent to which the Russians sought to intimidate their own population through atrocities. The inhabitants told the German military police that Russian security troops, before their retreat, had herded and whipped a large number of local boys between the ages of 14 and 17 years naked through the streets in intense cold.

Afterwards, they were said to have disappeared into where the NKVD had its headquarters, never to be seen again. During a subsequent search, all of the missing boys were found in a deep cellar, shot through the neck and covered with horse manure. The bodies were identified and claimed by relatives. Nearly all had frostbitten limbs...

In the face of the inexorable Soviet advance, von Manstein, commander of Army Group South, requested permission to withdraw. From Hitler came the predictable mantra: 'Kharkov must be held at all costs!' The Russians' 5th Guards Tank Army launched three head-on attacks on Raus's forces, which by now were forming the city's main defence. But they were not strong enough to hold the city and Hitler had no alternative but to give way. Raus was ordered to leave Kharkov on 22 August. The next day the city fell to the Red Army. During its period of occupation, the NKVD commandeered the former Gestapo headquarters, using the same basement torture chambers. Letterboxes were added so that citizens could denounce collaborators or betray others against whom they held grudges. Russian prisoners of war who were 'liberated' from a camp outside the city were close to starvation. As could have been predicted, these were mostly dealt with by the NKVD, who regarded them as spies or traitors. A good many were simply transferred from German POW camps to Soviet ones and to the GULAG.

From then on Soviet successes seemed assured. In the southern Ukraine, the advance was rapid. The entire German 17th Army of more than 65,000 men had been trapped in the Crimean peninsula. Further north, Smolensk was recaptured. Here, as elsewhere, the NKVD border guards went into overdrive. They established camps where troops drawn from even the lowest ranks of the Red Army were detained and accused of having been collaborators with the occupying Germans, who had discovered the mass graves of Polish officers shot within the forest of Katyn two years earlier when the Russians had controlled the area.

Stalin had broken off diplomatic ties with the Polish government–in–exile over the Katyn massacres. This served as a perfect pretext for moves in January 1943 by one of Stalin's most notorious henchmen, Pantaleimon Ponomarenko, First Secretary of the

Central Committee of the Communist (Bolshevik) Party of Belorussia and head of the General Staff of the Partisan Movement. His forces were marshalled to shower severe blows on small clandestine groups in towns and villages, together with individual AK cells and entire Polish guerilla units. He spelt out his intentions to Stalin, declaring that 'in the interest of the (Soviet) state we must undertake certain activities... Partisan struggle needs to be ignited in Poland. Aside from its military effects, it will cause serious losses among the Polish population resulting from the fight against the German occupiers.' Thus the weakened Poles would be unable to defend themselves. Time would then be ripe for a Soviet takeover. The Germans would do a lot of Stalin's work for him: shooting Polish prisoners once they learnt that they were the organisers of the various partisan groups. At the same time, Ponomarenko went on to stress that he regarded it as 'indispensable to send, in the spring, 80–90 diligently prepared and trained agents' to infiltrate the various underground movements.

The need for a second front

International attention was focused increasingly on the need for a second front and the post-war division of Europe. To this end, on 28 November 1943 a summit was held in Tehran, the first to involve 'the big three': Churchill, Roosevelt and Stalin. With some justification, Stalin, arriving after a flight escorted by twenty-seven Soviet fighters, felt he held the trump cards, not least because of his successes at Stalingrad and Kursk and his need to persuade the western Allies to take on a bigger commitment to combat the Germans and relieve the severe drain on his manpower.

At Tehran the operations of Beria's spies were remarkably successful. Present with him was his son, 19-year-old Sergo, who had been born in Tbilisi and worked with his father close to the apex of Soviet politics. In his later years he made an unsuccessful bid to clear his father's name and at his death in 2004 left behind numerous press interviews in a a biography, *Otets, Lavrenti Beria* (My Father, Lavrenti Beria).

With Lavrenti in Tehran in November 1943 and later in Yalta in

February 1945, Sergo's role was that of spy, closely observing Churchill and Roosevelt on their numerous walks:

> When the weather was bad, Roosevelt was wheeled in his chair and Churchill walked next to him, usually, and they always talked very extensively. And as we already had a system for directing the microphones to a distance of 50 to 100 metres to listen, as there was no background noise, everything was quiet, all these conversations recorded very well, and later on were translated and processed...
>
> My personal obligation was to listen to and record everything connected with Roosevelt and those close to him, to decode the recordings, and to report all this information direct to Stalin personally.

Each morning Sergo spent up to an hour with Stalin going over the intercepts of the previous day, performing a similar job at the Yalta conference. Additionally, he boasted that in Tehran 'we had a lot of agents and a network of spies', including agents who had infiltrated both the Russian and the English delegation.

By the year's end, the Soviet armies had progressed over 200 miles. History had gone into reverse: the Red Army, on a front stretching from the Black Sea to Moscow, had reached almost halfway to the 1939 border between the Third Reich and the Soviet Union. The German army had become the anvil upon which the hammer blows of the Red Army were from now on to prove merciless and unrelenting.

Chapter 7

Operation Bagration

Following the defeat of the Germans at the key battles of Stalingrad and Kursk, Poland dared to have its dreams of freedom. On 19 April 1943, there were uprisings in the Warsaw ghetto, put down with consummate savagery. Some 2,000 troops of the Waffen (armed) SS carried out major reprisals, including deportations to gas chambers and mass executions along with slow deaths in the network of labour colonies. The ghetto was bombed, shelled and burnt to heaps of rubble. Even so, the defenders held out until 16 May. Although currently available figures suggest that some 50,000 survived the internal destruction of the capital, their later fate at the hands of the Red Army and the NKVD will never be known.

However, the country remained in the mood for rebellion. At 5pm on a hot 1 August 1944, fighting erupted once more on the streets of Warsaw. The Polish Home Army (*Armia Krajowa*, AK) was one of the war's major resistance movements, led by General Tadeusz Bor-Komorowski, loyal to the London-based Polish government-in-exile and the country's largest underground organisation.

Formed back in 1942, it had absorbed most other Polish underground forces. Estimates of its membership at that time range from 200,000 to 600,000, but the commonly accepted number is 400,000, making it one of the two largest resistance groups in occupied Europe. But the AK, despite its successes in sabotaging German activities, was viewed by the Soviet Union as the main obstruction to its takeover of Poland. In August 1944 the AK launched an uprising, with the aim of liberating Warsaw before the arrival of Soviet forces.

At first the Red Army remained stationary on the Vistula, and watched the destruction of the city. It was widely assumed that Stalin's motive was to let the German army liquidate the Polish nationals, so that the Russians would not have to do it. However, it was later claimed that Warsaw had been beyond the grasp of the Russian forces anyway; their most advanced units were engaged in bitter fighting on the approaches to the city. Their advance was delayed until 20 September.

The Germans threw in elements of three new armoured divisions against the Russians outside Warsaw and the 1st Belorussian Front was driven back some 60 miles. German reinforcements poured into the embattled city under the command of the SS. Determined to drive them out, the Polish resistance poured thousands into the streets. For sixty-three days the battle raged in the cellars and the sewers and the number of those slaughtered soared to tens of thousands.

On 10 September, the Russians began the advance into the Warsaw suburbs. The NKVD was able to call on a score of well-equipped rifle regiments, buttressed by ample armour and artillery. Their men, and those of the Red Army, went into battle against the Germans fuelled with fear, knowing that at the slightest whim of a superior they could take a bullet in the back. But the Red Army had outrun its supply system and was obliged to gather its strength before assaulting the tough German defences around Warsaw.

Finally, on 2 October, when the Russians were unable to make the breakthrough, the Poles capitulated. Warsaw fell back into German hands, followed rapidly by all the villages and towns lying to the west of the Vistula. Over eighty per cent of Warsaw had been reduced to rubble by January 1945 when the Russians eventually entered the city.

Rotting dead

By then there were scores of dead rotting in the streets, while for those who had managed to survive there was only hunger and despair. If they felt hope at the prospect of the oncoming Red Army, it did not last long. Survivors throughout the country were regarded as traitors and collaborators and penal battalions were swiftly created. A rigid curfew was enforced between 2000 hours and 0500 hours, and the NKVD moved in, seizing all AK members and their supporters. By the winter of 1944–45, it was estimated that some 80,000 NKVD agents were operating within Poland.

Those Poles who had suffered first under the Gestapo now faced different techniques. Whereas one of the most feared sounds had been the approach of blaring sirens, the NKVD operated with stealth, its men dressing either in the uniforms of ordinary infantry officers or in plain clothes. Rather than being taken to a headquarters building which offered a tempting target, those rounded up for interrogation were taken to houses with anonymous basements from which many of them did not emerge.

In the meantime, reports reached London that wherever the Russians went in Poland, there were mass arrests of 'hostile elements' accused of collaboration with the Germans. To have been involved in any capacity with the Warsaw Rising was dangerous. At the end of August, the NKVD was ordered to detain and interrogate all Poles who had taken part in the rising and those who had managed to 'escape' into the Soviet part of occupied Poland. In Soviet eyes, they were spies. It was claimed that those held had been collaborating with both the English and the Germans to fight the Russians. The overall aim was to discredit the Home Army.

There were numerous cases of the sudden disappearance of AK personnel and the infiltration into the AK of NKVD propagandists. In some areas, attempts were made to organise military co-operation between the Red Army and the Polish formations for joint actions against the Germans. Polish commanders often as not found themselves arrested as double agents.

However, the Home Army remained a force with which to reckon. In the area of Radomsko in central Poland its partisan militia, still engaged in fighting the Germans, were commanded by Szymon Zaremba, who four years before had made his audacious escape from the NKVD.

Since the joint aims of my militia and the NKVD were combating the activities of the Germans during the Uprising,

I had been building up a network of local informers likely to have intelligence on possible moves by the Germans, so it was clearly essential for both sides to co-operate. My contact in the NKVD was a Major Gora, who commanded a small army of about 400 partisans. He agreed to work with me, but he was not the brightest of individuals, imbued with all the inbuilt NKVD suspicions of treachery around every corner. I foresaw likely problems and I was right. One of my most valuable agents, on his way to me with some potentially useful information, was trapped by Gora's men and swiftly shot. I was furious, pointing out that some crucial Intelligence had been lost irrevocably and demanded that Gora explain the action he had taken... His reaction was swift: 'The man was surely a spy for the Germans'. I pointed out that the agent's credentials had been tested before he was employed by us and if Gora and I were to work together it would be pointless in an atmosphere of perpetual suspicion.

After considerable argument, we hammered out an agreement that any detention in our area by the NKVD of a Pole had also to be reported to me. The man would then be questioned and if found to be an enemy agent would be forthwith shot. The agreement didn't hold for very long. Within days our men came across four Russian soldiers who, hiding after escape from a prisoner camp, were cut off from their units. They were clearly starving and before telling Gora about them, we saw that they were looked after and fed. But Gora's men lost no time in picking them up, not even bothering to interrogate them before they were shot. Gora was dismissive. 'I have quite enough men as it is. Besides I have no spare arms or equipment for them'. After that, workable relations were clearly impossible. Gora melted back into his own partisan unit and I later learnt that he had been killed in a skirmish.

Operation Bagration

Nobody in Russia was allowed to forget the summer that marked the third anniversary of Barbarossa. Above all, it was a day which had

(Left) Felix Dzerzhinsky (Iron Felix), creator of the Cheka, formed in December 1917 to launch revolutionary Bolshevism. He saw his task as hunting down and detaining 'the class enemy', a mission to be accomplished by 'solid hard men without pity'.

(Below) The obsessive revolutionary on the road to triumph. Vladimir Ilyich Ulyanov, otherwise Lenin, intent on securing the supreme power which led to the establishment of a twentieth-century totalitarian police state, advocating limitless methods of oppression 'to make the people tremble'.

Above) Alongside Stalin and Lenin in 1919 is another earlier revolutionary, Mikhail Kalinin, a former teenage agitator and Marxist factory worker who in that year became Mayor of Petrograd. He was careful to remain fiercely loyal to Stalin as Lenin's successor, emerging as a fortunate survivor of the Great Purges.

(Below) Held to be the world's most notorious prison, the late nineteenth-century Lubyanka building formed the headquarters of the Soviet police and became its foremost symbol of terror. Countless numbers of imagined or real opponents of the Communist system were periodically retained for interrogation, before being executed or shipped off to the GULAG camps. After the dissolution of the KGB, successor to the NKVD, the Lubyanka also became the headquarters of the Border Guard Service of Russia. It is currently one directorate of the police apparatus, the Federal Security Service of the Russian Federation (FSB).

Nicolai Ivanovitch Yezhov, the first ethnic Russian to head the NKVD with the title of People's Commissar of Internal Affairs. A mere 1.5m (5 ft tall) and known as the Dwarf, he was a super-efficient servant of Stalin.

On his disgrace, arrest and subsequent execution, Nicolai Yezhov, once enjoying the full trust of Stalin, forthwith became a non-person, subsequently wiped from all images. This was a common practice for leading figures out of favour, the most notable being Leon Trotsky.

The most able and the most sadistic of the NKVD leaders, Lavrenti Beria, short, balding and fleshy, enjoyed virtually absolute power within the Soviet Union during World War Two, as well as being chief executor of Stalin's Great Purges.

The bodies of thousands of Polish troops and civilians, shot in droves by the Red Army and NKVD in 1941 and deliberately blamed on the Germans were discovered by the Nazi invaders at Katyn in the spring of 1943. It took until 1992 before the Poles were handed the proof that Stalin had officially signed the original execution order, following a proposal by Beria to execute all members of the Polish officer corps.

Dating from 1930, the GULAGS – acronym for Main Administration of Camps – supplied pools of prisoners for the construction and maintenance of mines. Forced to achieve a high production quota, victims, drawn from every section of society, slaved in a brutal climate amid inhuman conditions.

A portrait of Stalin designed to convey the reassuring paternal image of the model statesman, in contrast to the reality of a ruthless dictator brooking no opposition and forever buttressed by intimidation, cruelty and terror.

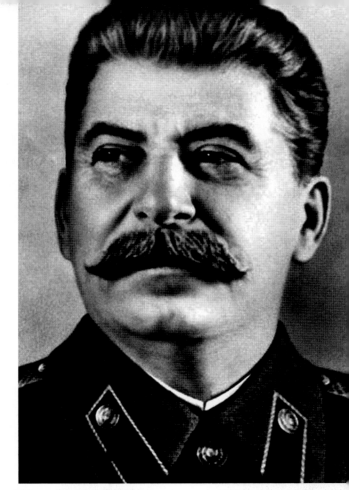

The great survivor, arrogant, purposeful Georgi Zhukov – nicknamed Zhuk, 'the beetle' – a peasant turned towering giant of the Red Army, hero of Moscow's defence, who rallied forces for besieged Leningrad and for the relief of Stalingrad.

Khrushchev, Stalin's successor, in his wartime role as a political commissar, photographed conferring with General Yeremenko during the Stalingrad campaign.

(Right) Viktor Abakumov, the OGPU veteran notorious as a specialist in torture and brutality and director of SMERSH (Death to Spies), was later held to be responsible for organising the murder of more than 4,000 of the murder victims in Katyn.

Forced labour was mustered as Moscow prepared for siege in the oncoming winter of 1941, so severe that it became known as General Winter, but which was to prove the capital's salvation. Some 60,000 Muscovites armed with spades, axes and shovels prepared to build fortifications to seal the city.

Red Army troops in the defence of a devastated Stalingrad. During the conflict the 10th NKVD Rifle Division carried out vital security and combat tasks within the front line.

Vlasov, tireless in his increasingly desperate anti-Soviet recruitment campaign, was only able to produce two divisions of doubtful strength in the defence of Prague at the war's end. By then he was nobody's friend, cold-shouldered by the Allies with their inflexible allegiance to Stalin. Vlasov was executed by those he betrayed.

belonged to Marshal Georgi Zhukov and the other Soviet commanders, whose massive armies erupted from the forests and bogs of Belorussia on 22 June 1944 to launch a bold surprise attack on the Wehrmacht's Army Group Centre.

The name for this operation tapped deep into Russian pride. It was called after General Petr Bagration, who in September 1812 had died fighting against the forces of Napoleon at the Battle of Borodino. Now, preceded by partisan attacks against Army Group Centre's key transportation points and air strikes, two successive offensives had spread over less than two months. The Red Army fronts, with 26,000 guns augmented by Katyusha rockets, pulverised the German positions. 4,000 tanks and 1.6 million soldiers took part in the Soviet attack. The end result was devastating for the Germans: their losses were calculated at around 1.5 million.

A preparatory role had been assigned to SMERSH, which had planted false intelligence with known German agents, claiming that the main attack was due to take place further south. It was a deception which led to Germany suffering what turned out to be one of the worst of its military disasters. Throughout, NKVD forces benefited from the equipment provided through the Lend–Lease agreement with the United States, including Studebaker and Dodge trucks. Towards the end of July they entered Lvov, in the western Ukraine, which with agreement from Germany the Russians had first seized in September 1939 and where the AK had struggled in vain to escape the Wehrmacht thrust.

Vyacheslav Yablonsky, member of an elite NKVD squad, was assigned a key role. The Germans still held Gestapo headquarters, so it was vital the building should be seized along with its contents, which included information that it was hoped would reveal the identity of those who had been key Nazi collaborators. While some of the force scaled the wall surrounding the headquarters, others had mown down the guards and prevented trucks stuffed with documents from leaving. Before long panic-stricken Germans, seeking to escape, made no attempt to protect their files, most of which were stored in the cellars. Papers revealed the identity of collaborators, who were swiftly rooted out. Yablonsky later declared: 'For saying something bad about the Soviet occupation the normal sentence was about fifteen years of hard labour.' Today, he admits: 'I think it was cruel, but I felt I was doing the right thing. I loved my country and I thought it was right.'

Enter Skorzeny

The Germans had made a desperate attempt to hit back. The sabre-scarred Austrian SS-Standartenführer Otto Skorzeny was involved. This flamboyant self-starred commando had made a name for himself by taking all the credit for rescuing Benito Mussolini from the latter's enforced exile in the Abruzzi Apennines, where he had been held after his overthrow.

The rescue was in the style of many of Skorzeny's exploits. Himmler had put his protégé in charge of a paratroop and commando school at Dahlwitz, near Berlin, which he staffed with handpicked pro-German Belorussian nationalists tasked with unleashing a guerilla war, backed by training in a clutch of specialities, including radio communications, encoding, sabotage and assorted methods of assassination. Before he and his men had been dropped behind the Belorussian front, Skorzeny, the eternal showman, staged a graduation parade for his successful recruits, collectively dubbed *Corny Kot*, Black Cat. They were led by General Michal Vitushka, a member of the Belorussian collaborationist government established by the Germans. At first, penetration of an unprepared Red Army rearguard was swift, but so was Russian recovery, aided by the presence of seasoned partisans, part of special forces units under the combined muscle of the NKVD and SMERSH.

Lucky to be among them, and to have survived the purges, was Dmitri Nikolaevich Medvedev, a one-time GULAG labour camp commandant from the Bryansk region. He had been suspected of dubious loyalty to the NKVD, from which he had been dismissed with ignominy, but he was subsequently reinstated. A born survivor, he went on to head partisan groups which carried out espionage, sabotage and assassination. The undercover name of his own partisan unit was Mitya.

An early triumph in September 1941, when the unit ambushed a German convoy, killing a general, had worked in Medvedev's favour, tripling his unit in size in just two weeks. Mitya leaders were soon forming other underground units, wreaking destruction on transport systems in the Bryansk, Orel and Mogilev sectors, and at the same time alerting the Soviet air force, whose bombers followed up with widespread demolition of stationary targets.

In June 1942, with a new unit, the Victors, Medvedev parachuted into one of the most dangerous occupied areas. That was Rovno in the Ukraine, where the notorious Erich Koch ruled. This former Rhineland railway functionary, under the patronage of Goering, had risen to Gauleiter of East Prussia, holding on to the title even when the Germans had taken over the Ukraine and later scooped up the provinces of Belorussia and the Bialystok forests. Koch boasted that he was the 'first Aryan to hold sway over an empire from the Black Sea to the Baltic'. During his brutal rule mass executions were carried out with his victims dangling on gallows erected in public parks.

Front line agents, who were working with the NKVD and were infiltrated into the Ukraine by Medvedev's partisans, killed more than 2,000 of the enemy, including eleven generals and high officials. At the same time they disposed of eighty-one freight trains. Medvedev's record gained him the title of Hero of the Soviet Union on 5 November 1944. At the war's end Erich Koch, with the recapture of the Ukraine, scuttled to East Prussia, hiding from the Allied forces until 1949 when he was tracked down by the British in Hamburg. He escaped revenge at the hands of the Soviet Union but was handed over to the Poles and given a life sentence.

Surviving German guerilla units around Belorussia in the dying months of the war were dispersed before they could do much damage to the partisans. Skorzeny's forces were shattered. A campaign of considerable brutality followed; large numbers of the population of Belorussia were scooped up and resettled in Siberia.

Operation Tempest

Earlier, the Home Army had conceived Operation Tempest (*Akcja Burza*), the chief aim of which was to allow Polish forces to seize control of German-occupied areas before the Red Army arrived.

The hope was that the Home Army could mobilise the local population into combating the Germans and that the Red Army would come to their defence.

Reports from resistance and partisan groups were telegraphed from Lvov Home Army district command (codenamed Wanda) to Major General Tadeusz Bor-Komorowski in Warsaw. This was a tortuous process, since there were no direct radio communications between district commands and Home Army headquarters. Radio messages were thus sent to Warsaw via the Polish command in London. Conflicting reports survive of the original strength of the Home Army in Lvov, which was put at between 3,000 and 7,000. At first there were successes and morale was high. Home Army forces had been divided into five districts, each with its own mobilisation centre. On 18 July, German civilian authorities and pro-Nazi Ukrainian militias withdrew from the city, followed by Wehrmacht forces, leaving just a token force. Large parts of the town were in Polish hands. But then fresh Russian divisions came up, bolstered by a tank brigade, and there were renewed street clashes.

The Home Army decided to switch its attacks to outposts heavily defended by the Germans. A Wanda report from Commander Draza Jugoslawianski and Captain Dragan Sotyrowicz informed Warsaw of the changing situation: 'A few hundred Home Army Officers are fighting for Lvov. Women and even children are involved in the fighting. One's hair stands on end at the sight of Poles facing the barrels of German sub-machine guns and being involved in street fights.'

For Colonel Wladyslaw Filipkowski, Commandant of the Home Army, there seemed an obvious solution: let his men be included in a full Polish division. At first the offer was accepted; then came the order from Moscow for the Home Army units to be disbanded forthwith. For Filipkowski there could be no resistance. According to a report from Wanda, NKVD forces arrived amid scenes of widespread destruction. From one AK centre had come the warning message for Warsaw: 'We fear arrests and torture in NKVD prisons.' The prospect was either to be forced to join units of the Red Army, or to be despatched to the GULAG. Filipkowski's fate was in the hands of Michal Rola-Zymierski, a main chancer who had thrown in his lot with Stalin and was later to be promoted marshal of Poland. Along with many of his followers, Filipkowski was arrested and sent to a succession of Soviet prisons and NKVD camps. There were additional arrests of those in AK centres who had stored weapons.

There was no end to the repression. Bor-Komorowski was receiving progressively gloomier accounts of everyday life from Lvov.

> Conditions are even worse than they were in 1939. There is no let up in constant searches and arrests. The Polish Bank has been closed and all its assets seized. Wages are not being paid, food supplies are not getting through and there is widespread looting of public buildings. Soviet bureaucrats are pouring in.

In the town of Kolomyia, Poles were driven out, while in Stryj, in the foothills of the Carpathians, there was compulsory conscription by the Red Army and an increasing number of females aged between eighteen and twenty-five were mustered for hard labour. By the turn of the year, widespread arrests had extended to the previously influential middle classes, notably university professors and members of religious groups.

A severe blow to Russian morale was the successful targeting, early in February, of General Nicolai Vatutin, a veteran of Stalingrad, who had gone on to lead notoriously aggressive forces against anti-Soviet Ukrainian peasant partisans. It had been known that Vatutin was scheduled to set out with an escort of heavy trucks and light cars to reach the town of Slavuta, where 60th Army had its command post. On the journey, the party branched off one of the major highways, making for a minor road, where it was obliged to slow down in sight of the awaiting Ukrainians.

An initial burst of fire ripped into Vatutin's car, setting it ablaze and severely wounding him. Then came the torching of a second. That was a cue for the guerillas, who had hidden out in the snow-covered fields, to surge forward; they were greeted by a riposte of machine-gun fire, which drove them back. Under cover of the fire, his men carried the injured Vatutin, heavily soaked in blood, and

made for the least damaged of their trucks but it was peppered with
bullet holes, and would not start. Eventually they came upon a
peasant with two horses and a sledge, on which they placed Vatutin,
journeying to make contact with a regimental doctor who swiftly
applied emergency dressings to the general's mangled foot. But his
life could not be saved; he died after being transferred to Kiev.

Throughout July and August 1944, Lithuania became a
battleground as the Red Army advanced towards Berlin. As early as
14 July, the forces of General Ivan Chernyakhovsky, smashing the
battered remnants of 3rd Panzer Army, had taken the capital Vilnius,
then Kaunus. According to AK reports, NKVD vehicles, streaking
through Vilnius, had paused long enough to throw onto the streets
the bodies of prisoners they had shot.

In a characteristically serpentine move, Beria had granted
Vilnius, with its substantial Polish population, a brief lull. This led
to a short-lived mood of euphoria; many of the inhabitants, enjoying
a false sense of security, had flown red and white Polish flags. But
those who had looked forward to solidarity with the Russians were
soon disillusioned, not least the city's eighty-year-old Polish bishop,
who had greeted the invaders with a crucifix in his outstretched
hands and was one of the first to be seized.

In overall charge of repression was the same Sergei Kruglov who
had graduated from organising the labour camp penal system, now
holding the rank of deputy minister of the interior. He was ordered
to co-ordinate a series of ruthless punitive measures, notably against
the partisans. The NKVD was heavily backed by infantry troops,
along with a highly efficient network of intelligence operatives and
informants, particularly in Vilnius where there were squabbles
between the partisan groups, many of which were deeply distrustful
of one another. Contingents of breakaway Lithuanians combined
with Ukrainian nationalists to pose as supporters of the Home
Army, infiltrating Home Army ranks. Another action by the NKVD
was a purge of religious communities suspected of offering
sanctuary to troops of the Home Army and collaborating with them.

Major Olechnowich of the anti-Soviet Polish underground
reported: 'There are ceaseless round-ups, arbitrary executions and
seizure of property. It is calculated that a minimum of 100 arrests

have been made from each countryside parish.' A major coup for the NKVD was a swoop on a Jesuit monastery and convent as well as the Church of the Holy Spirit serving the Dominican community. Discoveries included, besides weaponry, incriminating Home Army documents, printing equipment and uniform armbands, much of it hidden among the church archives.

At this time the NKVD instituted what the Soviets called the *istrebiteli* ('destroyer') programme. This involved selecting certain Lithuanian villagers and organising and equipping them to fight insurgents. Under NKVD pressure, each village was required to establish a unit of thirty men, who were bribed with food and ration cards and supplied with arms. Life proved particularly grim for those living in Koniuchy village in the Lida district, lying on the edge of the Rudnicki Forest, which was a base for Soviet forces carrying out raids on homes and property. In response, a campaign of self-defence was organised. On the night of 28 January various units of the Central Partisan Command in Moscow, including a fifty-strong group of Jewish partisans, surrounded the village. In the early hours of the following morning, when it was calculated that most of the inhabitants would be sleeping, a group of some 120 partisans, reinforced by men of the NKVD, tossed incendiaries into homes. Dazed families fleeing to escape were shot down. Elsewhere, in actions that foreshadowed the onset of the Cold War, prisoners who had survived the firing squads were rounded up for interrogation by the NKVD.

Ruthless firebrand

Defiant sections of the Home Army remained determined to fight back. On the night of 19 October 1944, actions against the NKVD and SMERSH focused on the small town of Ejszyszki in the Lida district of Poland's eastern borderlands. Lieutenant Michal Babul (codenamed Gaj) was a firebrand of considerable ruthlessness who, when it came to sealing the fate of his adversaries, was more than willing to go ahead without direct orders from his superiors. At Ejszyszki his object was to snatch key campaign documents from a senior SMERSH officer who was a captain notorious for capturing and routinely executing Home Army partisans.

Early intelligence reports received by Babul revealed that he could depend on a body of supporters who would spring into action in a bid to secure key Red Army posts, as well as residences housing Soviet police and military personnel. Other groups were hived off to take over key sectors, including a cooperative tannery building and mill, food and supply warehouses, residences housing NKVD men, military personnel and known or suspected collaborators. The SMERSH operative was eventually found holed up with guards in the home of Moshe Sonenson of the NKVD. Assault squads went in to snatch Babul's quarry, killing two Red Army men in the process.

No one had predicted a knot of inquisitive bystanders crowding in to witness the event. Casualties among them were inevitable. In addition, some of the AK squads had not been able to make it on time to their prearranged strike zones and were spotted by the Russians, making it impossible to capture earmarked local collaborators. It was reckoned, however, that the capture of the SMERSH captain made the exercise worthwhile.

But the NKVD, now reinforced by contingents within the NKGB, had not done with Ejszyszki. There were swathes of on-the-spot executions and arrests, and fugitives were rooted out. For Michal Babul, the adventure of Ejszyszki was his last hurrah. Along with some fifty others, he was arrested by the NKVD and shot.

Early in the following January, in a particularly bloody battle, also within the area of Lida, NKVD and SMERSH made numerous arrests among the partisans and their supporters. Many of the prisoners were deported to the GULAG. Soviet partisans had been able to turn the north-western Ukraine into a substantial base, but in the areas of Polesia and northern Volhynia, Ukrainian nationalists, under the banner of the Ukrainian Insurgent Army (*Ukrainska Povstanska Armiia*, UPA) had installed their own guerilla strongholds, whose insurgents focused on attacking Soviet lines of communication and the units of the NKVD. The tussle would continue at length.

Willing acolyte

Beria's acolyte Ivan Serov was in charge of mopping-up operations in Poland. He shrilly denounced the 'criminals and British agents' within the AK. Stalin had issued to Beria the notorious order 220145 calling for 'an immediate and energetic action against armed underground formations'.

Beria sought Stalin's permission to hand over to the NKVD, NKGB and SMERSH carefully selected officers from Poland who had 'operative value' – those with potential for collaboration. Others were directed to various NKVD camps 'lest they undertake the organisation of numerous Polish underground formations.'

Serov, in command of the Polish Ministry of Public Security, responsible for operations against partisan resistance, was particularly active in the Lublin area, south-east of Warsaw, which was the site of the notorious German Majdanek concentration and extermination camp. Here women, children and elderly Jews had been held pending despatch to the gas chambers. The victims numbered one and a half million within the space of a couple of years.

When the Germans were driven out in August 1944, Majdanek was taken over for the purposes of interrogation and torture by the NKVD. In charge was Belorussian commissar Lavrenti Tsanava, a dapper, black-haired Georgian Chekist, who was also in cahoots with Abakumov of SMERSH, whom Beria had brought to Moscow. This role was a fortunate break for Tsanava, who had previously been convicted of murder but was now considered ideally qualified for the job.

During December Serov was reporting to Beria that 15,000 AK members and affiliates had been detained there. Oppression was at its most vicious in the thirteenth-century Lublin Castle prison, where torture was routine. A clandestine underground newspaper revealed:

> It has been established that the NKVD and UB [Secret Police] torture their prisoners terribly at the Chopin Street [police headquarters] in Lublin... The most popular methods of extracting confessions include ripping off fingernails slowly, applying 'temple screws' [clamps that crush the victim's skull], and putting on 'American handcuffs'. The last named method causes the skin on one's hands to burst and the blood to flow from underneath one's fingernails. The torture is

applied passionlessly in a premeditated manner. Those who faint are revived with a morphine shot. Before the torture some receive booster shots. The torturers strictly observe the opinion of the chief interrogating officer whether it is acceptable to allow the interrogated to die. At the infamous Lublin Castle because of the injuries inflicted during interrogation, mortality among the political prisoners reaches 20 persons per week.

Beria's fresh concern centred on General Leopold Okulicki, Bor-Komorowski's successor, who on 19 January 1945 disbanded the AK, fearful that an allied force in Poland would encourage further Soviet oppression. Many units, though, elected to remain in place, supporting a new underground movement, armed with the military and radio equipment of the AK. As it turned out, there was plenty for them to do.

Reports, many in the form of telegrams from trusted locations, reached the government-in-exile in London, where they were quickly translated and circulated. One of these, dated 3 March, focused on events in the north-eastern district of Bialystok and in the district of Grodno in Belorussia.

In Bialystok:

... the NKVD is uninterruptedly carrying out the arrest of soldiers of the Polish Home Army and of all Polish patriots. During February 1945, 125 wagon loads of people arrested in the Grodno district and 242 wagon loads of people arrested in the Bialystok district were deported to Russia...

The arrested are kept in cellars, anti-aircraft trenches, underground lavatories, in the dark and are made to lie on the ground without any bedding. During interrogations they are beaten, tortured, starved, kept naked by the NKVD. The arrested men are accused of espionage for England and the Polish government in London, as well as collaboration with the Germans.

The mortality is very high. The commanders of the Polish army are deported into the depths of Russia and disappear without a trace. The NKVD frequently wears uniform of Polish officers. The NKVD has arrested all Gestapo narks and collaborators and subsequently released them and taken them over into their own service as their own informers.

The Russians have organised in town and all large settlements NKVD outposts for fighting the Polish Home Army. The Lublin Committee [in opposition to the government-in-exile] is collaborating with the NKVD so that the arrests among the Polish Home Army are increasing day by day.

When autonomous partisan groups became particularly active in Lublin, Beria and Serov sensed the need for swift action. Thus, in cahoots with Vsevold Merkulov, Beria's deputy, a trap was set that was vintage NKVD chicanery. In March 1945, with apparent friendliness and guaranteeing immunity from arrest, Serov invited Okulicki and seven key figures in the Polish resistance to fly to London in the company of a General Ivanov for a discussion on future relations with the Allies. All fell into the trap. There was no General Ivanov; on 28 March 1945 the party was flown to Moscow, the men going straight to the Lubyanka to be interrogated by Merkulov.

To many, the Moscow trial of the eight seemed like a re-run of the show trials of the previous decade. The proceedings were held in the capital's Pillared Hall, setting of the leading trials of the 1930s purges, and presided over by the same notorious judge, General Ulrich. During cross-examination, Okulicki made no attempt to conceal his motives and activities, admitting that he had fully intended to hold on to Home Army equipment which would be used 'against anyone threatening Poland', including the Soviet Union. He received a sentence of ten years, much of it to be spent in solitary confinement.

The activities of those still serving under the banner of the AK by no means ceased with the official ending of the war in Europe – VE Day – on 8 May 1945. Not the least of Home Army plans was to strive for the release of Emil August Fieldorf (codenamed Nil), who had fled an internment camp on the Slovak border and sped to France through Hungary, linking up with the newly-formed Polish forces-in-exile. He had then been smuggled back to Poland, where the NKVD seized him.

Irresistible challenge

News of Fieldorf's arrest presented an irresistible challenge to Captain Walenty Suda (codename Mlot), based in Minsk, whose agents lost no time in tracking their quarry to a notorious NKVD camp located in Rembertow on Warsaw's eastern outskirts. In the summer of 1941, the camp had been opened as the Wehrmacht's Stalag 333 for Polish prisoners. Eventually the Russians recaptured it and it came under NKVD control. Poles who had been held by the Nazis were among those who had been rounded up, because of Stalin's belief that they were traitors and collaborators. More than a thousand of them were destined to be transported to Siberia.

The conditions in the camp, later described by a witness, were known to be deplorable:

> Crush–Stink–Lice: and organisational chaos. Overcrowded, two–tier bunks would collapse, causing injuries and even fatalities... The numerous attempts at escape ended in volleys of gunfire and collective punishments. In short, not very pleasant...
>
> The lavatory was but one of many torments... It was designed for a few dozen people, but was supposed to be used by several thousands, many suffering from dysentery. Huge queues formed. Figures would squat all round the inaccessible building day and night, and the Soviet guards would amuse themselves by shooting at them. Many casualties ensued. (Every morning, the corpses would be carried along the ranks at roll-call for the purposes of identification).

Hunger and disease were rife, along with constant executions, after which corpses were buried in a collective hole in a nearby park. Intent on halting the flow of transportations, Suda set about creating a highly-trained unit of forty-four AK members, including partisans, under the leadership of Lieutenant Edward Wasilewski (codenamed Wichura), a flamboyant personality and a seasoned guerilla. In the guise of a member of the pro-Communist People's Army he set about scouring the approaches to the camp. Between its two fences with their thick tangles of barbed wire was a path stiff with armed guards and their patrol dogs. Towers sported NKVD marksmen touting machine-guns. Despite the ever-present risk of betrayal, Wichura went on to seek help from surrounding villages, securing the loan of trucks which, following an attack on the camp, would pick up sick and wounded prisoners for fast dispersal.

It was learnt that a day at the camp began at 6am, when a check was made on the number of prisoners. The day consisted of interrogations, tortures and mass burials in the park or in specially dug holes around the precincts of the prison. Planning for the attack was scrupulous. The men were divided into three groups. The first, led by Wichura himself, was to seize the gate, rush inside and open the barracks to free the prisoners, while the second group would eliminate the guards and the third group kept watch. The lightning onslaught, lasting some twenty minutes, started at midnight on 20–21 May, five days before the date set for the next transportation. The guards were taken completely by surprise. Around 100 of the prisoners were bundled into the trucks, while others were driven to forests and to villages where they were hidden. An AK despatch, sent to London, stated that the NKVD had lost fifteen dead, and witnesses said that as many as sixty-eight Soviet soldiers had been killed. Forty of the Polish prisoners attempting to reach the trucks were mown down by Soviet fire. The AK had no dead and just three wounded. In the confusion, it was hard to establish how many had been freed that night. The NKVD later admitted to 466, but the AK countered with a claim of some 800 men, pointing out that its force had also stemmed the flow of deportations.

Fresh Soviet forces, together with aircraft hunting for prisoners on the loose, headed for the area of Rembertow. As might have been expected, most of those they captured on the first day were Germans who were unfamiliar with the territory. Next day, things were different; the Soviets caught up to fifty men and shot them on the spot. When news of what had happened reached Beria he reacted with monumental fury and tightened security at other camps. The camp at Rembertow was closed.

Chapter 8

Rape of the Balkans

As the Russians advanced westward in 1944, Stalin and Churchill had agreed to slice up the Balkans into spheres of influence. Russia's intended regime of terror over the Baltic states had been spelled out in Order No.001223, termed 'On the Procedure for Carrying Out the Deportation of Anti-Soviet Elements from Lithuania, Latvia and Estonia', together with 'Enemies of the People', who could be anyone so defined by the NKVD.

Romania, along with Bulgaria, fell into the Russian sphere. For Hitler, it was a death knell. The Germans had originally entered the country in October 1940 when Hitler's adherent Ion Antonescu, a former cavalry officer and self-styled 'Conductator' (leader) had seized power. Now the former King Carol, forced to abdicate in favour of his eighteen-year-old son Michael, fled to Switzerland with his flame-haired mistress Elena Lupescu, having crammed as much royal booty as they could lay hands on into a royal train of nine coaches, including exotic pets from the royal menagerie. The train had sped on its way, accompanied by a fusillade of bullets from contingents of the Iron Guard, the most extreme of Romania's right-wing movements. The threat had sent Carol diving into a bath for protection. The party ultimately reached Lugano, where Carol eventually settled.

Power re-established

The Red Army went on to drive out out the Axis forces, establishing Soviet control over Romania, which had been one of its aims during the offensive. Hitler's main anxiety was economic: to ensure the protection of Romania's oil wells and installations at Ploesti, which provided an estimated one-third of Germany's wartime supplies of crude oil.

The Romanians put up a bitter struggle to stem the Soviet advance. The memories they had nursed were deep-seated and bitter. In June 1940 the country had been forced, under an ultimatum from the Soviet Union, to withdraw from its neighbouring territories of Bessarabia and Northern Bukovina. The Red Army and the NKVD moved in quickly, intent on the liquidation of those considered a danger to Soviet interests. Apart from strengthening border patrols, lists had been drawn up of families either suspected or known to have fled to Romania as 'traitors of the motherland', all of whom were earmarked for likely labour camp deportation. What happened was nothing less than wholesale slaughter. Killer squads focused on a succession of border villages, many of whose inhabitants made the crossing carrying white flags and religious symbols, and proved easy to pick out.

Figures for the death toll, later supplied by other villagers who survived, remain controversial and contradictory, but it was estimated that around 2,000 people were mown down by gunfire and many others wounded.

The centre of interrogation and torture was the NKVD headquarters at a commune situated at Adancata in northern Romania. Here it was later alleged that some of the captured wounded were tied to horses and dragged to previously excavated common graves where they were tortured and beaten with shovels, or taken to the Jewish cemetery to be buried alive with quicklime poured over their bodies.

Reaction to the Soviet incursions was often brisk, but retaliations were fatal. One of the first anti-Soviet groups was in Bessarabia. Opposition at the Vasile Lupu High School in Orhei was organised by students and some teachers. The town was a Jewish centre with a mix of Russian and Romanian speakers. At first the rebellion was relatively mild, restricted to writing anti-Soviet slogans in public places, including 'Death to the Stalinist occupiers', 'Go home barbarians', 'Down with the executioner Stalin', 'Bessarabia to Bessarabians' and 'Long live the Romanian nation'.

Behaviour became more provocative with the spread of anti-Soviet manifestos. Soviet red flags were removed and Romanian ones were put on top of the city hall at Orhei where the NKVD had its headquarters. There was a severe crackdown on the rebels and mass arrests and executions took place in Chisinau, which had been captured by the Red Army with the added muscle of three battalions of the 237th NKVD Regiment acting under Order No.00839. These troops of the NKVD raged throughout occupied Bessarabia. Their remit was to arrange the 'organisation of the evacuation of the population, evacuation of the prisoners and prevention of prisoner escapes.'

For the Romanians there was to be no relief, not even with the prospect of German defeat by the end of August 1944. In Jassy, to the north-east, the 2nd and 3rd Ukrainian Fronts encircled the German 6th Army; 200,000 of them were either dead, missing, wounded or prisoners. Army Group South Ukraine, which had consisted of two Romanian armies as well as the German 6th Army, had lost 400,000 men out of 905,000. A new communist government was set up in Bucharest, which was occupied on 31 August 1944.

Sharing in that success right from the early days was Alexandru Nikolski, one of the NKVD's fiercely dedicated operatives. Born to a miller in Chisinau, Bessarabia, he had joined the Union of Communist Youth, a wing of the Romanian Communist Party. This led to his arrest and a two-week incarceration by the Siguranta Statului (State Security). In December 1940, soon after the Soviet occupation of Bessarabia, he had been recruited by the Foreign Intelligence Directorate (INU) of the NKVD, and trained in espionage in Cernauti, which was at that time a Romanian province. His task was to penetrate Romania as an undercover agent and report on the movements of the country's army. No less vital for the NKVD was the need for information on the activities of the pro-German Romanian troops under the command of Antonescu.

The choice of Nicolski for this particular assignment turned out to be a serious blunder with elements of farce. Within two hours he was seized by frontier guards and his foreign identity revealed, not least because of his poor grasp of the Romanian language. With aplomb he passed himself off as an ethnic Russian but it availed him nothing. He was sentenced to hard labour and life imprisonment. Thinking ahead to the prospect of occupation by the Red Army, Nicolski, the ultimate survivor, swiftly planned his future with the communist controlled-government of Petru Groza. He lost no time in declaring allegiance to the notoriously brutal Siguranta Statului, ideal accommodation for an NKVD adherent, and his career prospered.

With the 6th Army decimated and the German 8th Army in retreat into the rugged Carpathian mountains, nothing stood in the way of the Russians entering Bucharest. The Ploesti oilfields passed to Soviet control; an anti-fascist coup effectively opened the way for the rapid advance of the Red Army into Hungary and threatened the collapse of the German eastern front. One Romanian army surrendered to the Russians and began to fight the Germans.

Soviet forces cleared Bulgaria and crossed Estonia's border, capturing its capital, Tallinn. The Estonian blue, black, and white ensign was again replaced by the red Soviet flag. Intense battles raged on the islands off the south-west coast until the end of November. The NKVD installed a network of guards along the coastline, seizing any boats that might be used by people who wanted to escape. Many Estonians fled to the forests and to Finland, but more than 2,000 were caught by the NKVD.

In the city of Tartu, in the south-east, the NKVD commandeered Gray House, a prominent apartment block at 15b Riia Street. Its owner, Oskar Somermaan, a prominent local businessman, was despatched with his family to Siberia. The grim history of this southern Estonian headquarters as the NKVD, which was used for interrogation and imprisonment, has made a deep impact on the country's psyche. Today visitors are taken along dimly lit corridors where a startlingly realistic wax figure of a uniformed Soviet interrogator emerges from behind a maroon-coloured steel door, while an inmate crouches in a tiny cubicle. Prisoners had to survive on half a litre of water during the first two days of interrogation. Prison cells and torture closets have been recreated in the building. Some 250 of those detained were shot, and their corpses were dumped into makeshift graves and the prison well. Individual exhibits in the museum still have a special poignancy: home-made wooden shoes worn by prisoners in the depths of a Siberian winter, five locks of blonde hair pinned to a handkerchief, which originally belonging to schoolgirls who had joined the underground movement and distributed resistance leaflets.

Former inmates return

In Lithuania, at the Genocide and Resistance Centre in Vilnius, memories of life there under the NKVD and later the KGB proved so profound that former inmates were unable to shake off their experiences and returned to act as guides. Many who had been brought there were tortured in the basement cells. Sleep deprivation was a favourite method of extracting information. In another basement cell used for interrogation the padded walls muffled the screams of victims.

In Tuskulenai Park in central Vilnius, evidence of savagery, conducted notably against partisans, was revealed in 2003, with the discovery of skeletons dating back to the rule of the NKVD. There were signs of torture – hands and legs had been severed – and of the strangulation of victims who had been strung up in town squares.

As for Latvia, the NKVD, under the iron control of the Latvian Commissariat of State Security, headed by Semen Shustin, had launched orchestrated attacks on the Latvian government. These had been followed by mass deportations during the night of 13 June 1941. Deportees were allowed only to take enough food for a month and were conveyed to the nearest railway stations, where the men were separated from the women and children. Shustin's orders were spelt out with chilling exactitude:

> In view of the fact that a large number of deportees must be arrested and distributed in special camps and that their families must proceed to special settlements in distant regions, it is essential that the operation of removal of both the members of the deportee's family and its head shall be carried out simultaneously, without notifying them of the separation confronting them... The convoy of the entire family to the

station shall be effected in one vehicle and only at the station of departure shall the head of the family be placed separately from his family in a car specially intended for heads of families.

Throughout their journeys, the trains were guarded by NKVD officers and a full military convoy. Barred cattle cars, with holes in the floor for sanitation, had been mustered for the deportees on their way to Siberia. Many died before the end of the journey and more perished in the first winter.

The NKVD did not loosen its grip on eastern Europe during the remaining weeks and months of the war. In Czechoslovakia Karl Hermann Frank, secretary of state in what was termed the Reich Protectorate, had in Prague faced a communist opposition growing more effective by the day. On 9 May 1945 the Red Army entered the capital, indulging in an orgy of raping and looting. Germans fled in collective panic, no longer safe on the streets.

Notorious turncoat

Along with the Soviet forces approaching Prague came agents of the NKVD and SMERSH, both with a specific mission, targeting a notorious turncoat. This was Andrei Andreyevich Vlasov, a peasant's son upon whom Stalin had showered an abundance of honours, including the Order of Lenin, the command of an armoured corps, the rank of lieutenant general, and the Order of the Red Banner for his role in the defence of Moscow. The command of the 2nd Shock Army had taken Vlasov to the front during the German assault on Leningrad. Bitter fighting in June 1942 resulted in complete encirclement with Stalin refusing to counsel any withdrawal; the shock army was annihilated. Vlasov, after taking refuge in a peasant hut, was captured by the Germans, and moved to an exclusive camp for prominent prisoners in the Ukraine, where Hitler had his forward headquarters.

It was here that there came the change of allegiance. As a student, Vlasov had attended a Russian Orthodox seminary, but a career in divinity in the wake of the 1917 Revolution had clearly not been an option. However, the malign methods of land collectivisation under Stalin and the sweeping purges of so much of the Soviet Union's leading military talent had bred in Vlasov a loathing of Bolshevism, and a desire to find a way of removing it. From his prison he wrote to the German authorities, proposing the creation of an anti-Stalinist Russian Liberation Army, appealing both to anti-Bolshevik sentiment and the population of the occupied area. It was a dream lofty in ideals but blighted by naive ignorance of Hitler's racial bigotry, which would not accept despised Slavs as allies. In addition, liberation for Soviet Russia was not on the Führer's agenda.

Ultimately realism was dictated by the inexorable advance of Soviet forces. At this point, enter Heinrich Himmler. The Reichsführer-SS was out to persuade Hitler that the promise of a free Russia might just persuade sufficient numbers of Russian soldiers to quit the Soviet ranks. Himmler and Vlasov met on 16 September 1944. An account of the proceedings was recorded by Gunter d'Alquen, an SS officer, who revealed that Himmler gave the go-ahead for the formation of the Committee for the Liberation of the Peoples of Russia (KONR) and for the publication of its manifesto, together with the raising of two divisions of Russians to be commanded by Vlasov. But this change of policy came too late.

At the conference at Yalta in the Crimea, held from 4–11 February 1945 and attended by the heads of government of the United States, the United Kingdom and the Soviet Union – 'the Big Three' – it was agreed that the Allies would repatriate Soviet citizens who had been captured by the Germans.

As a result the NKVD trawled through liberated German prisoner-of-war camps, searching out Russians who had been forced to join the German army and persuade them that they were regarded as loyal Soviet citizens with no need to fear for their futures. Others were quite beyond the reach of Vlasov and the KONR. They had been placed in special camps, ringed with barbed wire, and put to work as forced labourers, while the NKVD investigated their cases. In areas where it was known that those serving in the KONR had made inroads, a campaign was launched to discredit Vlasov as a traitor and tool of the Germans. Prisoners known to have been seized by the Russians were branded 'anti-Soviet collaborators' and 'Fascists'.

When it came to effectiveness, Vlasov's two divisions, fighting in March and April, proved pathetic; there was not the remotest possibility of them liberating a single individual in the east. Their presence also led to a dreadful irony. The men ended up fighting the Germans again, called to protect much of Prague from a rampaging SS force that was attempting to crush a Czech revolt. Hitler had continued to drag his feet when it came to supporting the liberation committee, refusing to accept obvious evidence that Germany needed every iota of support to save itself from the Russians.

Race to Prague

The Waffen SS also seemed blind to defeat. The fanatical Nazi Generalfeldmarschall Ferdinand Schorner of Army Group Centre had devoted a slice of his career to turning the Waffen SS from a paramilitary force into crack military stormtroopers to fight alongside the Wehrmacht. He had no inclination to give up now. Indeed, his troops were the last Germans to keep on fighting. In the early hours of 9 May 1945, the Russian 4th Tank Army raced to Prague.

In a vain attempt to evade the overpowering forces of the Red Army, Vlasov and his men headed south to surrender to the Allies. Vlasov was taken into American captivity and held in Tyrol. In talks with the Americans and British, he and his generals seized every opportunity to promote the principles of the liberation movement. It proved useless, since in no way would these two nations run the risk of crossing Stalin and disobeying their political leaders in alliance with him. The blunt truth was that Vlasov had become an embarrassment to the Allies. On 11 May, returning from talks with the Americans, his car was surrounded by Soviet troops, including armed contingents of the NKVD. His American escort did not intervene.

On arrest, Vlasov became prisoner number 31 in the Lubyanka, and was held there for a year along with eleven of his colleagues. At his first meeting with Abakumov the atmosphere was reportedly friendly, and Vlasov, softened up for interrogation, was treated humanely and given extra rations. But all too soon the mood changed. Abakumov had lost no time in stating that the twelve accused should be sentenced to death by hanging. The interrogations, deliberately lengthy and stretching over months, were carried out by Abakumov's deputy, Major General A.G. Leonov, head of the Department of Investigations. The Politburo approved the indictment and sentences.

By the time the trial, with its 38-page indictment, was underway with the ubiquitous Ulrich as judge, all the accused were seen to be drawn and fatigued. Although the proceedings were held *in camera*, a number of accounts were published, allegedly detailing Vlasov's confessions, in which he described his activities as 'counter-revolutionary' and 'anti-Soviet', condemning his colleagues as 'scum and dregs'. But since he had been under NKVD interrogation and possibly tortured, their value was clearly questionable. The newspaper *Izvestiya* reported that the prisoners were accused of treason and that as agents of the German espionage service they had carried out espionage and diversionary and terrorist activity against the USSR. All the accused admitted their guilt, and were condemned to death under Article 11 of the order of the Supreme Soviet; the executions were eventually carried out on 2 August 1946.

By the closing months of 1944 it seemed that nothing could stop the Red Army as it advanced towards Hungary, Czechoslovakia and Yugoslavia. Hungary proved Germany's most unwilling satellite, by March seeking to quit the war. In order to keep control of the country's oil wells, Germany launched Operation Margarethe, which led to the abdication of the regent, Admiral Miklos Horthy, and the setting up of a puppet government under a far-right dictator, Ferenc Szalasi, and his Arrow Cross Party.

This regime was short lived. By the end of the year, the Red Army had completed the encirclement of Budapest in preparation for a bitter battle. The accompanying NKVD went about their work with grim enthusiasm, arresting anyone considered even remotely likely to be guilty of war crimes or espionage or being anti-Soviet. The flimsiest of evidence, such as possession of a radio, was enough for the NKVD to make arrests.

Arrest of Wallenberg

With the presence of the NKVD it was certain that SMERSH could not be far behind. Most spectacular of its coups was the arrest of the Swedish diplomat Raoul Wallenberg, who in July 1944 had travelled to Budapest as the first secretary to the Swedish legation, where he issued so-called 'protective passports'. These identified their bearers as Swedish subjects awaiting repatriation and thus barred from deportation, and they were not required to wear the yellow star of David. The validity of these official-looking documents was nil, but they were generally accepted by the German and Hungarian authorities, partly because of bribery in appropriate quarters. The Russians suspected Wallenberg of exploring the possibilities of a separate peace between the Germans and Americans. In addition, since he was partly Jewish and from a wealthy Swedish family, he became an object of suspicion within the NKVD.

According to Pavel Sudoplatov, SMERSH authorities in Budapest passed details of Wallenberg's activities to Moscow, where Nikolai Bulganin, as deputy commissioner of defence, signed the order to detain Wallenberg, passing it on to Abakumov as head of SMERSH, who arranged for his quarry to be snatched from the streets of Budapest. Again according to Sudoplatov, Wallenberg's interrogation at Lefortovo prison and subsequently the Lubyanka had been accompanied by an invitation, inevitably spurned, to become a Soviet agent. Subsequently, on the instructions of Vyacheslav Molotov, People's Commissar for Foreign Affairs, and Andrey Vyshinsky, his deputy, instructions were given for Wallenberg's murder, carried out, it was said, by lethal injection. Sudoplatov's account was subsequently neither confirmed nor denied. A later claim that Wallenberg had died of a heart attack did nothing to stem a tide of rumours.

As for the siege of Budapest, it ranks as arguably the bloodiest of the entire war, rivalled if at all by the cauldron of Stalingrad. The Hungarian capital is divided by the Danube, with Pest on one side and Buda on the other, the high ground of which was captured by the Soviets on Christmas Eve. Two days later the city was encircled. From Stalin, the order had been stark: 'Take Budapest as quickly as possible.'

Red Army tanks burst into the Buda suburbs, whose hitherto peaceful streets became the battleground. German Tigers rumbed across the Danube to close with the advancing armour of the 3rd Ukrainian Front. At the same time, the 2nd Ukrainian Front of Marshal Rodion Yakovlevich Malinovsky was traversing the Danube above Budapest. The two formations joined west of the city. Five German and six Hungarian divisions, with some 800,000 civilians, were cut off and surrounded. Emissaries went forward to discuss capitulation terms. In Hitler's eyes, this was the ultimate heresy. There would be no evacuation. Budapest would have to be captured. The Russian riposte was a brutal rocket assault that tore apart the buildings and infrastructure of an ancient city, the noise only challenged by a cacophony of Soviet loudspeakers, urging the Hungarians to come out peacefully and throw in their lot with the Red Army. Those who decided to do so emerged only after pinning strips of red cloth to their uniforms. Those who did not were mown down.

Gabor Peter

At this time, security organisation in Hungary was undergoing drastic change. Gabor Peter (real name Benjamin Auspitz), a toothbrush-moustached Jewish tailor's assistant, had been working without complaint while Budapest crumbled around him. His job was a handy cover. Born in 1911, Peter had joined the Communist Party as a young man and attended training courses in Moscow, returning to Hungary quietly to build up his country's own security organ, to be known as *Allamvedelmi Osztaly* (AVO). Peter was answerable directly to the NKVD, who trained most of his men. Eventually, every Hungarian police precinct with an AVO section was ultimately responsible to its Soviet masters. Similarly, counter-intelligence officers were attached to each army battalion. Even so, Gabor Peter was not slow when it came to taking advantage of the situation. While Budapest was still under siege, his attention focused on Janos Kessmenn, a leading Hungarian Nazi with a record for exterminating Jews. Since it was no longer possible for his victims to be shipped to Germany, Kessmenn had, after relieving them of their possessions, lined them up on the Danube, where they were shot and their bodies tumbled into the water. Kessmenn, arrested by AVO, was assured that no action would be taken against him provided he handed over the booty stolen from his victims. He readily agreed, parting with $90,000 in foreign exchange, some 1,500 carats of diamonds, and over 10,000 assorted gold pieces, which enriched the coffers of AVO and the pockets of some of its members.

While the NKVD passed on to Hungary its trained agents and many of its methods, the Red Army broke down the German defences. The Hungarian oilfields located around Lake Balaton were beyond recapture by the Germans. The seizure of Budapest by the Soviets on 13 February proved the last major operation on the southern front for the Germans and the final offensive before the battle of Berlin. Hitler was reluctant to concede total defeat and launched *Unternehmen Frühlingserwachen*, Spring Awakening, aimed at winning back Budapest. The result was far from being an awakening: a spring thaw made the ground tough going for armoured forces. There were few gains. The Soviets went in with a swift counter-attack. German and Hungarian forces were finally thrown back.

By then, Gabor Peter's activities were being geared to more ambitious projects than machinations to undermine the Germans. His remit from the NKVD was nothing less than to sabotage Hungarian plans for a democracy. A nationwide network of informers, ordered to seize dissident politicians, oversaw mass arrests of citizens who either ended up in the GULAG or were shot. In this climate of terror, reinforced by the continued presence of the Red Army, the Hungarian republic broke apart.

The invasion of Austria was spearheaded by Marshal Fyodor Ivanovich Tolbukhin, a veteran who had commanded an army at Stalingrad. His troops pressed ahead to the Danube and Vienna, relentlessly slaughtering anyone in their path. On 13 April 1945 Vienna was secured. Ahead lay the offensive in East Prussia.

To meet Soviet manpower demands, more than one million prisoners from the GULAG were transferred to the Red Army. Lurid accounts were cited of 'terrible atrocities of the German bandits', which could now be avenged. Home propaganda focused on liberated prisoners from German camps who were full of 'burning hatred for the enemy'. But their casualty rate was appalling; many of them, pale and undernourished from their treatment in the GULAG, were scarcely candidates for survival and had no experience of combat.

As for the NKVD, its troops continued to comb bombed-out towns for truant soldiers masquerading as civilians. A manifesto, said to have been written by Ilya Ehrenburg, the Soviet Union's prominent propagandist, was circulated among the troops. It ranted:

> Kill, Kill. In the German race there is nothing but evil!... Follow the precepts of Comrade Stalin. Stamp out the fascist beast once and for all in its lair!... Kill as you storm onward, kill! You gallant soldiers of the Red Army.

In January 1945 an increasingly desperate Himmler once again called in Otto Skorzeny, who was at this time in command of a group of specialists in anti-partisan assignments. Skorzeny was ordered to infiltrate a team into the rear of the Red Army in Poland to disrupt Soviet supply routes. The troops disguised themselves in Romanian army uniforms with the insignia of a specialist unit. The journey east started in East Prussia, going on through more than 500 miles of enemy territory. They aimed to join up with other groups, but these had already been infiltrated by the NKVD, which launched a large-scale cordon and search operation. From the Soviet rear areas, Skorzeny's men were forced into ignominious retreat. Few survived.

On 15 April 1945 Hitler fulminated against:

> ...the deadly Jewish Bolshevik enemy... Soldiers of the East! You are already fully aware now of the fate that threatens German women and children. While men, children and old people will be murdered, women and girls will be reduced to the role of barrack room whores. The rest will be marched off to Siberia...

Increasingly isolated, the Führer took refuge in the delusion that Germany would still win. Stalin's armies launched their final offensive acoss the Oder. Zhukov, Konev and Rokossovsky held the principal commands. Zhukov's 1st Ukrainian Front was in constant touch with Stavka, but it was on a leash: the 108th Special Communications Company of the NKVD was present at his HQ, controlling and monitoring all his communications with Moscow.

Beria saw to it that the deputy to each front commander should be from the NKVD – Serov and Tsanava for the 1st and 2nd Belorussian Fronts and General Pavel Meshik for the 1st Ukrainian Front. Stalin's power, exercised through Beria, was absolute. Reminders were ever-present. There was a flood of propaganda anticipating the Soviet triumph which referred to 'Our great genius and leader of troops, Comrade Stalin, to whom we owe our great victory.' To challenge that 'genius', even by implication, was an act of supreme folly and extremely dangerous. Stalin's vaulting paranoia, fed by Beria, stalked the one million Red Army troops as they advanced on a crumbling Berlin.

Chapter 9

Anarchy in Berlin

From early in 1945, the advance on Berlin became a roller-coaster. At the end of January, Soviet forces in Silesia had been within 250 miles of the capital. On the same night, troops further north had pushed beyond the 1939 Polish frontier town of Rawicz, going on to secure the final bridgehead. Berlin was about to be declared a fortress city.

If the mood was one of elation on the way to a certain victory, one man did not share it. Marshal Constanin Rokossovsky, commander-in-chief of the 1st Belorussian Front, had dreamed of the glory of taking the capital. The post had been snatched from him and given to Zhukov in what he regarded as a humiliating disgrace. Instead, Rokossovsky was in command of the 2nd Belorussian Front, entrusted with the attack on Prussia, which had nothing of the kudos he had craved. He still carried bitter memories of his appalling experiences as a victim of the purges, when he had been arrested and had nine of his teeth kicked out by the NKVD. He had also suffered broken ribs and smashed toes. After his release from four years in the GULAG had come promotion to general and despatch to a Black Sea resort to put on weight and be measured for his new uniform. Of equal importance had been a visit to a dentist noted for his discretion who had fitted Rokossovsky with a set of steel teeth.

There had been one recent incident that had reminded him sharply that he was still being shadowed by both the NKVD and the counter-intelligence echelons of Abakumov's SMERSH, both following hard on the heels of the Red Army. He had been present during an incident of humiliating retreat by some troops who had been reduced to wearing tattered uniforms shorn of insignia and weapons. Unwisely, he had commented: 'Tomorrow all our papers will be reporting on the heroic withdrawal of the Red Army.' A SMERSH lieutenant within earshot had given him a sharp warning: 'You are out of prison now. Do you want to go back?'

Beria at this time continued to use every opportunity to prove his loyalty to Stalin and boost his career chances. The increasing role of SMERSH had led Abakumov to divert his attention from debauching young women and beating prisoners with rubber truncheons. In place of such self-indulgence, he was edging his organisation towards adopting key roles within the 12,000-strong NKVD forces attached to invading army groups. His very presence and what was seen as his interference were particularly resented by those troops who had grown weary of what seemed a long war. His representative within the 1st Belorussian Front was vested with draconian powers. Every man in the front line had to submit to a thorough investigation of his loyalty to the extent of monitoring even the most seemingly innocent conversations in off-duty moments.

The Red Army's next offensive would burst over Germany's eastern marches. Stavka proclaimed that there was a score to settle:

> Comrades! You have reached the borders of East Prussia, and you will now tread on that ground which gave birth to those fascist monsters who devastated our cities and homes, and slaughtered our sons and daughters, our brothers and sisters, our wives and mothers. The most inveterate of those brigands and Nazis sprang from East Prussia. For many years now they have held power in Germany, directing foreign aggression and its genocide of other peoples.

A heavy NKVD presence was there to ensure 'the elimination of spies, saboteurs and other enemy elements'.

In towns and villages, terror was unleashed, notably at 0700 hours on 22 October 1944, where 11th Guards Army, reinforced by the NKVD, which was maintaining security in the rear of the advance, captured and butchered the Prussian village of Nemmersdorf. Goebbels sent crews to film mutilated corpses of women and children. The films were widely shown in German cinemas, although it was later alleged that footage from other locations had been included to enhance the propaganda value.

Target Königsberg

The ancient city of Königsberg, known as 'the citadel of East Prussia', was home to a German garrison and scores of civilians, many of whom fled ahead of the Red Army's advance, particularly as word spread about the fate of Nemmersdorf. Constant air and land attacks were merciless. Crucial to the destruction were the soldiers of 3rd Belorussian Front, commanded by General Ivan Chernyakhovsky, one of the brightest stars of the Red Army. The front advanced into Königsberg, which had been declared a fortress (*Festung*), often covering fifty miles a day, reaching the fiercely defended city in January 1945. Hitler Jugend personnel and members of the SS took refuge in civilian homes or merged into columns of refugees, hoping to escape detection. The NKVD's main concern was that no one should escape, declaring: 'Encircled soldiers in Königsberg are putting on civilian clothes to get away. Documents must be checked more carefully in East Prussia.' The siege of Königsberg was to rage all through February and March and by April, Stavka was reporting: '...During the Red Army's advance on the territory of East Prussia, NKVD representatives removed from January until April this year over 50,000 enemy elements.'

Königsberg's streets were strewn with chunks of masonry, smouldering vehicles and the carcasses of horses and human beings. Its commandant, General Otto Lasch, disillusioned by the appalling cost, had been anxious to capitulate. But, deaf to all reason, the fanatical SS, with the staff officers of 69th Infantry Division, had opted to fight on. Erich Koch, the East Prussian gauleiter, roundly denounced any capitulation and set about ordering troops and *Volkssturm* (national militia) to form resistance groups. Response came from the NKVD special detachments, some of whom were still approaching the city. Entire districts were ripped apart and areas were left devastated for years. In acts of wanton destruction, civilians were driven from homes that at first had been reduced to rubble and then set alight, while farms that had been attacked had all their livestock slaughtered.

According to an NKVD report in early February, there was general panic:

> The bread ration has fallen to 300 grams for soldiers, 180 for civilians. Some of the inhabitants want to surrender, but many have been frightened by Goebbels' propaganda, and of the coming of the Red Army. On 6 February, the corpses of some 80 German soldiers executed for desertion at the north railway station were found bearing signs: 'They were cowards but they still died.'

The civilian population was herded into forced labour for fifteen to sixteen hours a day in forests, bogs and canals. Victims of mass rape were nailed to barn doors and farm carts. In the west and north-west of the city flame-throwers and Molotov cocktails set buildings alight; their defenders fought to the death. It was all ultimately fruitless. General Lasch surrendered the remnants of his forces on 10 April, to end what he later described as 'the senseless sacrifice of further thousands of my soldiers and civilians... I therefore resolved to cease fighting and put an end to the horror.'

About 50,000 residents (compared to Königsberg's population on 1 January 1940 of 372,270) remained in the ruins of the city. Hitler's reaction was as expected. In Berlin, Lasch was condemned to death by hanging *in absentia* and his family arrested under the Nazi *Sippenhaft* law, which decreed the arrest of the closest relatives of traitors to the Nazi cause. The family survived the war, while Lasch was later wounded and captured by the Soviets.

After seizing Königsberg, the next move of the Red Army was to secure the vital ports of Danzig and Stettin, and here all vestiges of restraint were swept aside. Even as the fire from Russian aircraft swept onto the columns of retreating German troops, forces of the Wehrmacht and the SS seized stragglers at random, hanging them from the nearest trees. Troops of the Red Army behaved no better, indulging in an orgy of riot and looting, leading to the admission from Major Fyodor Romanovsky of the NKVD: 'It was very difficult to maintain order as we advanced into Germany.' It proved impossible for the Germans to hold on to Danzig. It was estimated that 10,000 German prisoners were taken, but the number of deaths was infinitely greater. Nothing could stop the victorious march of the Red Army across shattered central Europe.

Stalin, meanwhile, had another anxiety. He had become increasingly worried about the possible future actions of the Poles, in particular the 1st and 2nd Polish Armies, currently fighting at the side of the Red Army. But for how long? His suspicion was that these forces could be intent on eventually declaring their support for the government-in-exile in London, of whom he had been obliged to make some recognition following the 1941 German invasion. Stalin had agreed then to the formation of a Polish army from prisoners in Russian hands, which was to be commanded by General Wladyslaw Anders, who in June of that year had been released from Soviet captivity to form Polish contingents to fight in uneasy alliance with the Red Army.

To feed Stalin's anxieties, the NKVD and SMERSH were put to work. Beria eagerly acquired a report from Serov, referring to the development of an increasingly 'hostile attitude' and 'unhealthy moods', particularly in the 1st Polish Army towards the Red Army. SMERSH lost no time in lining up informers prepared to detail the activities of Polish soldiers said to be regular listeners to 'the London radio' and who believed that no fewer than three million of Anders' men were intent on entering Berlin alongside 'the English army'. Other informers claimed that England and America had plans to help the Poles get rid of the Russians.

None of this stemmed Stalin's ever-present obsession with the hunt for traitors. So extensive were transportations of suspect Soviet citizens that the GULAG buckled under the strain. Conditions within the camps deteriorated rapidly and their staffs were unable to cope. Those who dared to plead to Stalin for the numbers of prisoners to be reduced were at best ignored or at worst detained.

Fate of the Cossacks

Even harsher treatment was reserved for those who had served in Cossack regiments, drawn from people of southern European Russia and adjacent parts of Asia, including Muslims, who had a long military tradition as loyal cavalrymen during Tsarist times. Many had fought against the Bolsheviks in the civil war, crossing over to serve with the Germans, greeting the incursion of the Nazis into villages and farmsteads, singing local anthems and bearing gifts of food and flowers. Vengeance was decreed by Abakumov and SMERSH in obedience to Stalin's policy of forcibly resettling 'unreliable peoples', seen as potential Nazi collaborators, and their allies. Furthermore, local Muslims were also accused of close ties with Turkey, the ally of Nazi Germany, and conspiracy against the Soviet Union.

The most notorious case of forcible repatriation of Cossacks happened during May and June 1945, involving some 50,000 people, including 11,000 women, children and elderly men. Homeless at the war's end, they had retreated to western Austria. Among those who were prominently in the sights of SMERSH was a group of former White Army generals, two of whom, Pyotr Krasnow and Andrei Shkuro, were known to be in Austria, where a SMERSH detachment was despatched with orders to detain them. They had, however, quit their camp in the village of Gleisdorf, leaving the Soviet agents to interrogate Shkuro's mistress, Yelena, who revealed that the men had applied to the Allied commander, Field Marshal Alexander, for protection. Eventually unearthed, the Cossack officers were told that they were to attend a conference with Alexander where their fate would be decided.

The invitation had all the hallmarks of a SMERSH scam, which was precisely what it was. There was to be no meeting with Alexander. For the ageing Krasnow and three others there was capture by SMERSH and the NKVD, followed by all the horrors of torture, imprisonment in the Lubyanka and death by hanging. Other high-ranking officers and enlisted men either perished in the labour camps or were released after Stalin's death in 1953. Few ever succeeded in reaching the west.

Elsewhere, in a camp near Lainz, to the west of Vienna, a group of Cossacks, some of them accompanied by their families, were herded onto bridges. The NKVD waited as they were forced to cross and mowed many of them down. Mothers threw their infants over the sides of the bridges; then jumped themselves. There was the spectacle of one man killing his entire family and laying the corpses neatly on the grass before shooting himself. During the widespread imprisonments in Austria, victims were incarcerated in iron cages at Spittal, then handed over to Soviet security forces at Judenburg, the Soviet zonal frontier. A disused steel mill became a centre for firing squads.

As the Red Army marched across East Germany, the NKVD saw to the construction of what were termed 'special' concentration camps – *spetslagerya*. Two of them were prepared quickly: these were at Sachsenhausen and Buchenwald, the sites of former Nazi concentration camps. Prisoners housed there were destined to be totally neglected. One of the most notorious camps was at Furstenwalde, east of Berlin, where there is a memorial to some 4,000 people who died of starvation and disease. They came under the direct control of the NKVD, which had plenty of experience of organising similar camps in the GULAG back home.

Secret decrees

Early in the year, the tireless Beria had formulated secret decrees, detailing categories of people he considered should be arrested and delivered to the camps. These were members of any profession whose members dared to question Soviet authority. Besides military commanders, these included police and concentration camp personnel, the more influential public servants, newspaper editors and 'other enemy elements'. Emphasis was given to the need for 'Chekist measures' against 'spies, diversionists and terrorists', including those who had been placed by the Germans behind Soviet lines.

The NKVD never rested. Day and night, summary arrests were made in East Prussia, Pomerania, Posen and Silesia. Victims, prior to being deported to the Soviet Union, were incarcerated in newly established internment camps. After the German capitulation, the extent of arrests widened, taking in civilians, including the elderly, women and children, who had scarcely been convinced Nazis.

Within Berlin, there were groups who were destined to be severely disillusioned by Soviet rule. Communists, who had been either trapped or imprisoned by the Germans, looked forward to the day when their liberators would arrive. Often, even under the watchful eye of their captors, the more militant had been organising cells whose members were entrusted with compiling detailed dossiers on their SS and Gestapo tormentors. Their intention was to hand these over to their 'liberators' in the hope that this would give them an easy passage.

Particularly zealous was a cell in the Neuenhagen-Hoppegarten sector, east of Berlin, which had gone as far as drawing up detailed plans for what it believed could be the future administration of the area. Their hopes were soon to be dashed. The NKVD and SMERSH were fully aware of Stalin's unwavering distrust of any groups who had experienced long-term contact with the enemy. This was nothing new. As far back as July 1941, when the war in the east had barely started, he had ordered 'that men coming out of German encirclement should be rigorously investigated by the NKVD Special Sections to root out German spies.'

At interrogations those held were bombarded with such questions as 'Tell us how long you have been collaborating', or 'tell us for what purpose the Gestapo sent you here!' They were questioned as to why they had not set up groups of saboteurs and partisans. Such neglect was frequently defined as 'counter-revolutionary crime'.

To be a German was in itself an act of treachery. In one instance, it made no difference to the fate of a German woman picked up by the NKVD who had been working for Soviet partisans as a translator. She was deemed to have been 'aiding and abetting the enemy' and was sentenced to a ten-year *katorga*, from the Greek word *kateirgo*, meaning 'to force'. Throughout its history, the NKVD had not scrupled to draw on the practices of the officially disowned Tsarist empire. In the early eighteenth century, Peter the Great had mustered convicts and serfs to build roads, fortresses, factories, ships and much of St Petersburg itself. In 1722, Peter passed a directive which ordered criminals and their families into Siberian exile.

As repression mounted in the territory captured by the Soviets, in beleaguered Berlin, General Helmuth Reymann, Commander, Berlin Defence Area, signed the 'Basic Order for the Preparations to Defend the Capital'. Hitler's bombastic rhetoric was manifest in every clause. Defence was to be 'to the last man and the last shot'. The battle was to be fought 'with fanaticism, imagination; every means of deception, cunning and deceit'. Each defender was to 'be filled with a fanatic desire to fight, that he knows the world is holding its breath as it watches this battle and that the battle for Berlin can decide the war... Every block, every house, every hedge, every shell hole was to be defended to the uttermost.'

Battle for Berlin

At precisely 4am on Monday 16 April, the battle proper for Berlin began. Less than thirty-eight miles to the east of the capital, red flares burst in the night above the swollen River Oder, prefacing a mighty artillery barrage. Six days later, a crucial Russian assault began. The city had already been pounded into virtual oblivion by Allied bombing, a process accelerated by guns, rockets and tanks. An area of more than eleven square miles was reduced to a sea of rubble. Of Berlin's 1.5 million homes, over 600,000 were obliterated. Thousands of dead bodies lay unburied: there was an all-purveying stench of putrefying flesh. In such drinking water as there was, lay the seeds of typhoid, diptheria, tuberculosis and dysentery. Medical attention was a mere gesture: 4,000 people were dying each day.

The inexorable advance of the Russian forces did nothing to stem the distrust and rivalry between the NKVD and the Red Army. The NKVD spurned allegiance to the military chain of command, an attitude which had been particularly prevalent during the earlier storming of the Oder. In the army the feeling was that there should be no needless obstructions in the onward march to Berlin. But too often the NKVD was obsessed with clearing occupied territory of 'hostile elements', leading to the wasteful deployment of scores of NKVD troops, who could have been more useful in battle areas.

This situation had done nothing to stem Stalin's insatiable demand to be kept fully informed of what was happening in the centre of the capital. General Ivan Serov, the same inflexible Stalinist who had been a prominent figure in the conquest of the Baltic states, perceiving threats to his own security, installed cordons in and around the city, consisting of men from 105th, 157th and 333rd NKVD Frontier Guards Regiments. They and their fellow frontier guards were among the great survivors from the earliest days of the Soviet Union, created during the time of the Cheka. Their forces of elite manpower had faced particularly fierce combat in the first weeks of the German invasion of the Soviet Union. Now they were in charge of a city which contained dwindling numbers of enemy troops and crumbling defences.

By the time of his marriage to Eva Braun and their suicide on 30 April, Hitler had been installed in his thirteenth and final headquarters (*Führerhauptquartier*, FHQ, the Führerbunker), an elaborate complex of shelters into which were huddled eighteen cramped, low-ceilinged rooms. Links with the outside world had dwindled to a switchboard more suited to a modest hotel: one radio transmitter and one radio telephone link with OKW headquarters at Zossen, fifteen miles to the south of Berlin. The depressing daily conferences had been held in the bunker's passageway, so narrow that it could scarcely hold all those who had to be present. With the Russians within striking distance, Hitler's weakening grip on reality had become even more marked. Hours had been spent pondering a model of what had been intended to be the post-war rebuilding of his home town, Linz. Either that, or he had crouched, mesmerised, by a treasured portrait of his idol, Frederick the Great.

Within the capital defence was, in essence, provided by the 1st Flak Division, just six battalions and miscellaneous SS and police. To those Russians who had fought their way across Europe since 1941, nothing had demonstrated more starkly the impending Nazi defeat than the calibre of opposition facing them in the April days four years later.

Confronting the NKVD were, for the most part, boys as young as sixteen and men as old as sixty who had been pressed to serve with the Volkssturm. This consisted of some twenty battalions, for the most part untrained. As a last resort to boost fighting strength, the Volkssturm had been formed in 1944 when General Heinz Guderian, chief of *Oberkommando des Heeres* (Army Supreme Command) called them up when he had been shorn of the manpower he desperately needed to stem the growing Russian advance. They had no designated uniform. In essence these men and boys became the German equivalent of Britain's Home Guard, the so-called 'Dad's Army.' But unlike the Home Guard, they were expected to fight on the front line. After the war, the commanding officer of the 42 Volkssturm Battalion in Berlin recalled:

> I had 400 men in my battalion, and we were ordered to go into the line in our civilian clothes. I told the local Party leader that I could not accept the responsibility of leading into battle without uniforms. Just before commitment we were given 180 Danish rifles but no ammunition. We also had four machine guns and a hundred Panzerfausts [anti-tank weapons]. None of the men had received training in firing a machine gun, and they were all afraid of handling the anti-tank weapons. Although my men were quite ready to help their country, they refused to go into battle without uniforms and without training. What can a Volkssturm man do with a rifle without ammunition? The men went home; that was the only thing they could do.

A veteran of the Grossdeutschland Panzer Corps, who encountered a Volkssturm battalion, recorded his impression of the young boys:

> They had been hastily dressed in worn uniforms cut for men, and were carrying guns which were often as big as they were. They looked both comic and horrifying, and their eyes were filled with unease, like the eyes of children at the reopening of school. Not one of them could have managed the impossible ordeal which lay ahead... We noticed some heart-wringing details about these children... Several of them were carrying school satchels their mothers had parcelled with extra food and clothes, instead of schoolbooks. A few of the boys were trading their saccharine sweets which the ration allowed to children under thirteen.

Throughout, the soldiers of the Volkssturm proved easy targets, receiving no mercy whatever from the NKVD rifle regiments. The Wehrmacht turned its back on them, supplying no arms or equipment. Elderly men in these units were decked in patched uniforms and children sported coal-scuttle steel helmets. The only common issue item was an armband in lieu of a uniform. After uttering their oath to Hitler, these tyros were flung into battle. Even battle-hardened Wehrmacht and SS, encountering boy soldiers on the way to battle, pleaded in pity: 'Go home, it's over'.

To Serov's NKVD frontier guards, they were simply traitors. The elderly, useless in attack or defence, were 'saboteurs and terrorists' and as often as not were shot on the spot. Small children found playing with Panzerfausts, which they regarded as toys, were rounded up.

The Wehrwolf

The mission of the frontier guards was also to root out a fanatical group which Himmler had established in the autumn of 1944. Even though there was the ever-increasing reality of ignominious defeat, Himmler, the moon-faced Reichsführer-SS, despite being happiest in his cosy refuge in the past, was forced to recognise that a conventional fighting force had a limited role in the face of the rapid advance of the Allied forces. He became wistfully attracted to the notion of the Wehrwolf, inspired by a novel set in the Thirty Years War by Herman Lons, an extreme nationalist killed in 1914 and a figure revered by the Nazis. Thus came the creation of *Unternehmen Wehrwolf*, a resistance movement dedicated to sniping and sabotage. Himmler declared: 'Even in territory which the enemy believes they have conquered, the German will to resist will again and again flare up in their rear, and like Wehrwolves, death-defying volunteers will injure the enemy and cut his lifelines.'

The Wehrwolves were under the command of SS-Obergruppenführer Hans-Adolf Prutzmann, whose links with the Nazis went back to the days of the Freikorps. These were paramilitary units which had been formed during the Weimar Republic that was created at the end of the First World War and destroyed with the advent of Nazism. He had been a student of Soviet partisan tactics during service in the Ukraine, progressing to become a highly efficient butcher, who by the middle of 1941 was forcing Latvians into the ghettos of their major cities, seizing their property and ultimately murdering most of them. Prutzmann was designated General Inspector for Special Defence, and backed by

Goebbels, who proclaimed: 'We Wehrwolves consider it our supreme duty to kill, to kill and to kill, employing every cunning and wile in the darkness of the night, crawling and groping through towns and villages like wolves, noiselessly, mysteriously.'

Otto Skorzeny was given command of Wehrwolf groups under the banner of the SS Jagdverband (hunting teams). Soldiers and civilians, under the orders of the SS, were to be schooled in sabotage, liquidation of enemy agents, poisoning food and water supplies and attacks on transport.

The staff headquarters was established at Schloss Hulcrath, a castle near the Rhine town of Erkelenz, where the first 200 trainees, Hitler Jugend adherents, arrived in late November. Skorzeny's men gave intensive lessons in sabotage, small arms, survival and radio communications. Fieldcraft lessons were hard and brutal. In darkness, foxholes had to be built and on completion were inspected. If any of them were inadequate those who had been responsible for their construction were beaten. Prutzmann also set up training centres in the Berlin suburbs and in Bavaria. In addition, special bunkers were prepared for the use of those members of the group operating behind the lines and were stocked with supplies and munitions. Ahead of attacks on selected Soviet positions, secret caches were provided with weapons and three months supply of food. Units behind the Soviet lines, equipped with explosives, radio transmitters and carrier pigeons, sent warnings of Russian advances back to the German defenders.

Other initiatives included training in the production of home-made explosives and the manufacture of detonators from everyday articles such as pencils and cans of soup. It was intended that every member should be trained to enter a guard tower and strangle a sentry in one swift movement, using string.

In the years following the war, there was a growing tendency to talk down the effectiveness of the Wehrwolves. Widely quoted was General Siegfried Westphal, the last German Chief of Staff in the West, who when captured in May 1945 had contemptuously dismissed them as a 'rabble of boy scouts'. But in fact, their existence had attracted the attention of Allied intelligence and was greeted in some quarters with alarm. An intelligence summary by Supreme

Headquarters Allied Expeditionary Force (SHAEF) had concluded that:

> The main trend of German defensive policy does seem directed primarily to the safeguarding of the Alpine zone... Air cover shows at least 20 sites of recent underground activity...
>
> Ground sources have reported underground accommodation for stores and personnel. The existence of several reported underground factories has been confirmed... In addition several new barracks and camps have been seen on air photographs... Reports of extensive preparations for the accommodation of the German Maquis-to-be are not unfounded.

Savage riposte

The response of the NKVD to the Wehrwolves was predictably savage. During the winter offensive in Poland and East Germany, members of a ten-man Wehrwolf group had been surrounded by an NKVD patrol east of Nielkoppe and all but eliminated. In another incident in the Vienna woods, to the west of the city members of a uniformed Wehrwolf rearguard were butchered and their bodies mutilated.

One of the prime tasks of Wehrwolf groups operating in north-eastern Austria was to report on Russian troop movements along the roads, specifying types of guns, tanks and other arms. One incident involved a Wehrwolf road-watch detail dug in on the forward slope of a hill, overlooking a road near Bruck an der Leitha in eastern Austria. A Red Army column drove past, headlights blazing. For a while the group, dug into its foxholes, was undetected. Then, suddenly, tanks broke away from the column, reinforced by NKVD in the rear, and swerved towards them, coming on in line abreast, firing their guns and driving over the foxholes, crushing the occupants.

There were no scruples, either, when it came to mowing down members of Hitler Jugend, a group largely formed of teenagers, which from the 1930s had mushroomed into a mass movement.

Within the Volkssturm, the Hitler Jugend was employed for reconnaissance purposes, entrusted with giving early warning as Russian forces ploughed through Germany's eastern provinces. During February 1945 Hitler Jugend teams had been flung into the cauldron of the besieged city of Elbing, in northern Poland, where, touting pistols and in civilian clothes, they had been seized by the NKVD.

The methods of retaliation employed by the Wehrwolves went way beyond the accepted tenets of conventional warfare. Poisoning of enemy food and drink supplies proved highly effective. In one incident, troops of the 3rd Belorussian Front found a barrel seemingly containing harmless spirits, but which had been treated by the Wehrwolves. At first there were no ill effects. But within two days seventeen men had died in agony. One NKVD directive fulminated:

> Since the German animals are not in a position to halt the all-destroying onslaught of the victorious Red Army, they fall back upon the dirtiest, basest, and most hideous means of warfare, such as the poisoning of alcoholic drinks, water and food. The German monsters reckon that if they succeed in eliminating our soldiers and officers, they will inflict losses on the Red Army and weaken it... Always keep in mind the danger of poisoning! We do not want to offer the despicable enemy even the smallest chance to do us harm or poison our people.

Right up until the official end of the war and beyond, the presence of large numbers of such men in the woods around Berlin posed severe problems for the Red Army. There were incidents of Wehrmacht deserters being infiltrated by groups of Wehrwolves, intent on offering armed resistance. It was not long before Wehrwolves were being held responsible by the NKVD and SMERSH for just about every semblance of resistance. Those members of the group rounded up were handed over to SMERSH and many were either executed or sentenced to life imprisonment in Siberian camps and mines.

There were cases where those carrying out arrests received the aid of former Nazis happy to betray their fellow Germans in the vain hope that this would save them from arrest. Additionally, SMERSH agents resorted to blackmailing their prisoners into helping hunt for SS and Wehrmacht officers in hiding. Sniffer dogs penetrated apartment blocks and even allotment sheds, which were being used as places of refuge.

The NKVD and SMERSH directed German communists in Berlin to identify both 'enemies of the people' – their political opponents as well as former Nazis – and those deemed 'loyal to the Soviet occupation'. Enemies of whatever hue were left in no doubt as to their fate. Furthermore, there was no scruple when it came to adopting one deep-seated Nazi practice. This was the system which used wardens and receptionists to watch over every street, house, apartment block and hotel. There was no shortage of takers; wardens merely carried on with the work they had being doing under the Nazis.

One quality that the NKVD had in abundance was patience. Several years after the war's end, NKVD agents conducted extensive sweeps through the occupied Soviet zone, intent on winkling out Wehrwolf agents still at large.

With some degree of irony, the continued existence of Wehrwolf, Volkssturm and associated splinter groups provided useful material for Soviet radio propaganda. Despite the obvious impending defeat of the Nazis, and for the benefit of home listeners, NKVD propaganda continued to be deliberately exaggerated. It was emphasised that the Russians were facing a formidable foe and that the Red Army was clashing with 'German bands up to 1,000 strong'. The truth was often prosaic – scattered Volkssturm had ambushed trucks, motorcyclists and carts simply to seize food wherever they could get it.

In Berlin itself, there were increasingly few regular troops. For those that were there, ammunition was in short supply. Neither was there much sign of the Luftwaffe; Soviet aircraft had a clean sweep of the skies. On 20 April, Red Army salvoes were hurled into Hermannplatz, in the south-west of the city, killing those queuing outside Karstadt's department store. Exploding shells could be heard in the area of the Chancellery and tanks were rumbling through the suburbs.

SMERSH personnel were put under intense pressure by Stalin, who demanded to know whether Hitler was alive or dead and hinted at hideous penalties for the slightest suggestion of inaction. When the Chancellery was reached, the initiative was seized jointly by Beria and by Abakumov, who sent in his 3rd Shock Army to search the building. Neither man was in the mood to share the credit; Zhukov and the military authorities were kept out of the picture, along with those troops who had taken part in the capture.

Hitler's suicide

Huddled in a jeep and dodging a spate of shells, the shock army contingent had to find its way through streets so strewn with rubble as to be virtually unrecognisable. Maps proved totally useless. Since all road signs had been destroyed, drivers were obliged to edge their way with the help of passers-by. On the day the Red Army reached the Reichstag, the newly married Hitler shot himself in the bunker with his Walther 7.65 calibre pistol. His long-term mistress Eva Braun took cyanide. Witnesses testified that the two bodies were carried up to ground level through the emergency exit and taken to the small, bombed-out garden, where they were doused with petrol and set alight.

In accordance with Hitler's last will and testament, Joseph Goebbels, the Minister for Public Enlightenment and Propaganda, became the new 'Head of Government' and Chancellor (*Reichkanzler*). On 1 May, within hours of Hitler's suicide, Goebbels despatched General Hans Krebs, Army Chief of Staff, to Chuikov's headquarters under an agreed flag of truce, in a bid to negotiate a partial surrender. The encounter between the two men took place at 4am. A rambling Krebs, delivering Goebbels' terms in the grip of fatigue, got precisely nowhere.

A call outlining the encounter was made to Zhukov, who insisted that Stalin be contacted at his dacha. His reply survives: 'No negotiations except for unconditional capitulation, with either Krebs or any others of Hitler's lot.' Krebs returned to the bunker empty-handed. In the early hours of 2 May he was soused in brandy. He and an equally sozzled General Wilhelm Burgdorf, formerly Hitler's chief military adjutant, blew their brains out. A renewed and ferocious Russian barrage bombarded the Reichstag and the Chancellery. By then Magda Goebbels had poisoned her six children and then committed suicide with her husband.

The first Russian combat troops entered the bunker without opposition; the quest for Hitler's body was underway. Resentment in the Red Army had already flared, since authority for these troops had been hijacked by the NKVD, under the eager leadership of Colonel Ivan Klimenko, a specialist interrogator whose first action had been to locate Goebbels' corpse and take it back to his headquarters in Berlin's Ploetzensee prison. Further digging in a crater revealed the charred remains of a man and a woman and two dogs, spotted at first by a private, Ivan Churakov. Klimenko assumed that what remained of Hitler's cadaver was in the Chancellery. Only later did he realise the possible significance of what had been unearthed. No credit was given to Churakov for the initial discovery. That was seized by Klimenko, who gleefully secured the decoration of Hero of the Soviet Union.

The announcement of Hitler's death, interrupting the strains of Beethoven's 7th Symphony, had been broadcast from Hamburg radio on the evening of 1 May. It was accompanied by two stark falsehoods, one stating that Hitler had died 'fighting to his last breath against Bolshevism', the other that he had been at his Chancellery command post. Most Berliners remained in ignorance; a sizeable slice of the capital lacked electricity and radio reception was impossible.

A week later, on the day of the Nazis' final capitulation, Berlin was flooded with bizarre rumours. Far from being dead, Hitler, it was claimed, had scurried to safety through the tunnels of Berlin. On the contrary, it was declared that he was safe in American-occupied Bavaria, where he had been smuggled by air. Other claims were made that the Führer had made for Spain by submarine and thence had fled to the Argentine. An item by the Soviet newspaper *Izvestia* declared he was alive and living in a moated castle in Westphalia. Here was a calculated dig at the British: Westphalia lay within the British occupation zone.

For Stalin, many of the rumours had welcome propaganda value.

It was suggested that the British or Americans might be hiding Hitler and would do a deal behind Russia's back. At a press conference held on 10 June, Marshal Zhukov declared 'We do not have any mortal remains that have been identified as a corpse of Hitler'. This was nothing less than the truth, since Zhukov had been kept firmly in the dark.

Crucial evidence

At the same time, a small band of SMERSH operatives had the task of positively identifying the Führer's remains. News on the radio of the Nazis' final capitulation on 8 May reached Elena Rzhevskaya, the team's young interpreter from Moscow, then at Karlshorst, on the edge of Berlin. The capital was in the grip of fevered celebration, but Rzhevskaya was in no mood to share it. She clutched crucial evidence: a small red satin-lined box entrusted to her by Colonel Gorbushin, containing flesh-specked jawbones extracted from Hitler's corpse. Many years later, when the allegedly full details emerged, she declared:

> Can you imagine how it felt? A young woman like me who had travelled the long military road from the edge of Moscow to Berlin, to stand there and hear that announcement of surrender, knowing that I held in my hands the decisive proof that we had Hitler's remains. Only two officers knew what I was carrying and I had to keep my tongue.

Despite everything, she had been caught up in the general euphoria, pressed on one occasion to dispense wine to colleagues while still clutching the vital box. Hitler's dentist was eventually tracked down. The identity of the jawbones was confirmed in the presence of Rzhevskaya and two of her superior officers. The autopsy also revealed both gunshot damage to Hitler's skull and glass shards in the jaw.

Even at this stage, SMERSH was reluctant to leave well alone. A new figure muscled in, determined to establish personal authority. This was General Pavel Meshik, Deputy Head of the Main Counter-Intelligence Directorate. In circumstances that could scarcely have been more macabre, the remains were repeatedly buried and then, at Meshik's demand, dug up for a series of re-examinations. The caskets were then laid in a grave at Magdeburg on the River Elbe. But in the eyes of Moscow, there was a danger that Hitler's legacy would last. Yuri Andropov, who was to become director of the KGB, destined to become the NKVD's successor, was dogged by fears that any burial site could become a shrine to neo-Nazism, and he swiftly ordered the final destruction of the remains. Their ultimate fate is still in dispute. According to some accounts, on 4 September 1970 a KGB team exhumed the bodies of Hitler and his wife and burned them before dumping the ashes in the Elbe. It has also been claimed that the ashes were flushed down the town's sewage system.

Even this was not the conclusion of a grim saga. According to research by the British historian Antony Beevor, Hitler's jaws, which had been in Rzhevskaya's red box, were retained throughout by SMERSH, while the NKVD hold on to the cranium. Both were recently discovered in Soviet archives.

The search for Hitler's corpse and the question of whether he was alive at all had become a matter of indifference to thousands of Berliners mired in poverty, huddling in cellars and air-raid shelters. Homes that had once been secure no longer existed. Every third house had been destroyed, while three million cubic feet of debris littered the streets.

Where anarchy ruled

Elsewhere in the capital anarchy ruled. The NKVD was incapable of rounding up Russian deserters who in more ordered times would have been shot on the spot or snatched for the GULAG. Soviet troops brazenly roamed the streets, looting whatever they could find and frequently stealing cars from under the noses of the British military guard. Clothing of all kinds and in almost any condition was at a premium, fetching sky-high prices on the black market. Women arriving at the railway stations had valuable property, particularly fur coats, taken from them. When it came to gathering intelligence about the administration of west Berlin, the NKVD did not scruple at detaining German civilians working there and subjecting them to prolonged interrogation, on occasions holding them for weeks and months.

Beria continued to assure Stalin that anyone deemed to have been guilty of collaboration was being arrested, many Russians among them. Released NKVD figures reveal that as early as October 1944, 359,590 Soviet troops who had been prisoners of the Germans fell into the hands of the NKVD. Of these, SMERSH creamed off some 36,700. The addition of suspects from eastern Europe and the Baltic states appreciably swelled the population of the GULAG between 1944 and 1945. In Moscow, by way of contrast, fevered victory celebrations took place on 9 May 1945, topped by a bibulous banquet at Zhukov's headquarters.

Across Europe, though, the mood when the Yalta conference had been in progress back in February had been very different. In Britain, intelligence throughout the war had been in the hands of the British Secret Intelligence Service (SIS), working closely with the Special Operations Executive (SOE). This was known as Station 43 and was used as the principal training school for SOE's Polish Section between 1942 and 1944. Those running SOE were particularly anxious to gauge the morale and learn of the future plans of the Home Army command network. This was in a state of flux since Bor-Komorowski's surrender to the Germans. Any hope that he might lead a new uprising was over and he had been sent to the fortress prison of Colditz.

Operation Freston

This situation prompted a daring British-run partisan initiative, dubbed Operation Freston, which was fraught with danger. Four British agents were to be parachuted into western Poland. In command was newly promoted Colonel Marko Hudson, a seasoned resistance fighter who in Yugoslavia had run a network of saboteurs, specialising in destroying Axis shipping in Dalmatian ports.

Inside Poland, a special role had been assigned to Szymon Zaremba, whose job was to act as a courier passing information back to the Polish government in London. Since he was already a marked man with the NKVD he had gone under an assumed name. On arrival in Poland, the group was to seek out contacts who could come up with detailed evidence of the Soviet plan to dominate the countries they occupied, including Poland.

On 26–27 December 1944, the group landed close to the fighting lines at Czestochowa, lying north-west of Krakow. They dodged a German platoon with the aid of AK forces before being overrun by Soviet advancing troops, who bundled them into a jeep and drove them to a nearby cottage. Here they introduced themselves as British officers keen to work with their Russian allies and with the Poles against the Germans. At first their reception was friendly, save for one officer, a marble-eyed colonel from the NKVD, who accused them of lying: the men could not be Allied soldiers because they had contacts within the Home Army which consisted of bandits, collaborators and war criminals.

Documents and identity papers cut no ice: the colonel had sneeringly pointed out that these could easily have been forged by the Germans. Hudson stared out his interrogator, refusing to answer any questions except to an officer of his own rank or above, and ordered the others also to be silent. The result was deliberately calculated humiliation. On the orders of the NKVD the team was hustled into what had been a notoriously oppressive Gestapo prison with three-tier bunk beds whose straw mattresses were alive with vermin. Szymon Zaremba later recalled: 'Within five hours of being there, I was lousy with lice.'

Conditions worsened. Troops urinated and defecated in the building in which the captives were held. Halls, stairs and passages were heaped and spattered with piles of excrement. Access to toilets was denied for 24 hours, food was rye bread and an unpalatable gruel of warm water with a few grains of barley, all of which was delivered in a filthy bucket. The glare of a light bulb kept the inhabitants of the cells awake all night. In temperatures well below zero, the men were hustled to a latrine, which had been placed over a shallow trench. A small mercy was two packs of playing cards which the men were given in their cells.

Meanwhile, at Yalta, Russia had gained everything she wanted, including sealing the fate of Poland. It seemed likely that the Soviets, by holding the Freston participants, had prevented much information from reaching the western powers at a critical time. Soon the presence of the Freston prisoners clearly became an embarrassment for the Soviets. In a diplomatic move, they were released from the clutches of the NKVD and were able to make their way to the considerable comfort of the British Military Mission in Moscow.

But even then they were not free from the NKVD. They were under constant surveillance and were not deceived by seemingly friendly social invitations, which were seen as highly suspect overtures and firmly refused. A simple cover story had been mapped out: each man had been a prisoner of war and had been liberated by the Red Army. Eventually they were granted visas and left for home to report to SIS and SOE on Russia's almost certain plans for what was to become the Cold War.

Chapter 10

Towards the Cold War

At the time of the victory celebrations in Moscow, Beria approached Stalin with a proposal draconian even by NKVD standards. He recommended a further hardening of the repatriation campaign that had begun in the autumn of 1944. At Yalta, both the British and the Americans had accepted the agreement, knowing full well that repatriation meant certain death or captivity. All Soviet soldiers liberated by Allied forces on German territory and repatriated were suspected traitors and were incarcerated in camps, some in Poland. Many were summarily shot by the NKVD on their arrival by sea, either at Odessa or Murmansk. Many went straight to the GULAG in Siberia.

Such treatment was remembered with considerable bitterness by the arch-dissident Alexander Solzhenitsyn, who in 1973 published *The Gulag Archipelago* and wrote:

> These were the defenders of their native land, the very same warriors whom the cities had seen off to the front with bouquets and bands a few months before, who had then sustained the heaviest tank assault of the Germans... And instead of being given a brotherly embrace on their return, such as every other army in the world would have given them, instead of being given the chance to rest up, to visit their families, and then return to their units – they were held on suspicion, disarmed, deprived of all rights, and taken away in groups to identification points and screening centres, where officers of the Special Branches started interrogating them, distrusting not only their every word but their very identity.

When it came to organisation, the repatriation programme, to all appearances, could not have been in better hands. Scarlet-faced, squat and balding, Colonel General Filip Golikov might well have emanated from central casting as a precise model of the hardened professional soldier. In addition to having an irreproachable record as a combat commander in the Moscow, Stalingrad and Voronezh campaigns, he was a briskly efficient organiser, ideally suited to head the board of the bureaucratic Main Administration for Repatriation of Soviet Citizens, better known as the Soviet Repatriation Commission. But as far as politics went, he was a mere cardboard cut-out. The real responsibility for repatriation was in the hands of the NKVD, SMERSH and the NKGB, which had a parallel function to collect intelligence.

Agents were infiltrated to work alongside the incumbent repatriation officials. Displaced persons were bribed, blackmailed and threatened by methods of thuggery more suited to the sidewalks of Chicago. One defector, a turncoat former employee with SMERSH, later related:

> Some agents were bought for money, others paid in service to us for their own ill-calculated drunkenness and moral depravity. We used special female personnel for this... [Others] might be promised complete forgiveness for all past sins and an honourable homecoming to their Motherland. They might also be threatened with reprisals and of course threats would be made against their families, if they happened to be in Soviet hands.

Another tactic was orchestrating a propaganda campaign to woo western opinion and to encourage hitherto reluctant individuals to return home. Beguiling appeals were circulated with leaflets, one of these declaring:

> The mother country remembers its children. Not for a minute did the Soviet people, our government, or the party of Lenin or Stalin forget about the fate of Soviet citizens who temporarily found themselves under the yoke of Fascist oppression.

Films, designed to stir feelings of homesickness, were widely screened and the NKVD did not hesitate to fabricate letters from relatives, describing how safe conditions were in the Soviet Union.

After Germany's defeat, there was chaos and uncertainty, in Europe, and in the Far East the war against Japan was still going on. It was agreed that the three principal wartime allies should meet at Potsdam, in the southern suburbs of Berlin, which had been the setting just twelve years before of a ceremonial handshake between President von Hindenburg and Hitler, then the new German Chancellor. Potsdam was heavily scarred by Allied bombing. A date, 15 July, was agreed. Stalin, sensitive about his safety and wary of air travel, declined to make the journey by Dakota, opting for rail. The Soviet leader turned out to be the only survivor from previous conferences: Harry Truman, following the death of Roosevelt that April, had succeeded as US President, while Churchill withdrew when he lost Britain's General Election in early July, to be replaced by Clement Attlee.

Surviving trappings

In planning Stalin's arrival, Beria had no scruples when it came to pressing into service elegant surviving trappings from the time of the Tsars, in this case four handsome green railway carriages hitched to a total of eleven heavily armed coaches. The route was lined by 17,409 NKVD troops. An additional eight armoured trains were prepared. Eleven aircraft maintained close links with Moscow, while three others were at Stalin's disposal. All surrounding stations and airports were trawled for likely 'anti-Soviet elements'. And the NKVD supplied its own fire brigade.

Sixty-two villas were appropriated for the Soviet delegation and these were defended by seven regiments. Stalin, resplendent in a white high-coloured tunic with burnished epaulettes and the status of Generalissimus, was met on arrival by Zhukov, who had chosen for the conference, due to last until 12 August, the imposing Cecilinhof, former palace of the Russian royal family. As it turned out, Stalin was a day late, fuelling rumours that he had suffered a minor heart attack, a symptom of his deteriorating health.

Stalin's belief that deadly enemies surrounded him persisted.

When he went for a garden stroll, NKVD guards were present in considerable numbers. Platoons of troops sported sub-machine guns, while Stalin was flanked throughout by Beria's men. He was not permitted to walk for more than a few hundred yards before being picked up by car.

On the surface fresh peacetime collaboration between the Allies appeared possible, with bitternesses and rivalries consigned to the past. Reality was otherwise; Potsdam turned out to be the last conference of Allied leaders. Britain and the United States were suspicious of the motives of Stalin, who had already installed communist governments in the central European countries under his influence. The political temperature was beginning to cool rapidly. Agreement on Allied aims for the demilitarisation and de-Nazification of Germany was straightforward enough. Russia, however, remained inflexible in the face of calls for free elections and the restoration of human rights in the countries it had occupied.

The Poles suffered harshly. The communist-controlled military organisation in Poland was backed by the Russians, effectively spelling the end of recognition for the London–based Polish government-in-exile. Moscow gained control of almost forty per cent of Germany's post-war area, thirty-six per cent of its population and thirty-three per cent of its resources.

The prospect of repatriation did not attract all the Russians who found themselves in western Europe at the end of the war. In the former Dachau concentration camp some Soviet prisoners-of-war committed suicide rather than go home, and deserters from the Soviet forces were pursued by the NKVD. Soviet citizens, originally from the Baltic states, who had managed to escape from Germany to Sweden, were returned to Russia, since the Swedes were fearful of Russian retaliation.

Indeed, Russians who were in German hands at the end of the war had almost nothing to look forward to. A Lieutenant Dlynnich, an officer who had been captured by the Germans, later revealed his fate. He had been put to work in a factory near Berlin and was wounded by an exploding mine. He was in hospital when Soviet forces liberated the region.

After my recovery I was sent to a screening camp and thence to a construction battalion. In the screening camp all the Russians who had been in Germany had to appear before a commission of the NKVD. A detailed interrogation took place. How, why, and when did you get to Germany? Why didn't you join the Partisan movement? Where and with whom did you work in Germany, and so forth. Beatings are frequent. All those suspected of collaboration with the Germans (be it only on the basis of denunciations and hearsay) are sent to separate camps and then appear before the Revolutionary Tribunal in Frankfurt-on-the-Oder where after a brief trial they are sentenced to various terms of forced labour in concentration camps – usually more than five years.

Younger men and some of the women were despatched to construction battalions. Those who were older with children were sent home. This was not a passport to freedom, however. The adults were required to report to NKVD local offices, followed by a two-year sojourn in a special labour camp. Repatriates, especially those who had been in the American or British zones, were denied the full benefits of education and forbidden to take up responsible positions. Precisely how long such a ban was in force was entirely at the whim of the authorities.

Displays of enterprise and bravery shown by captured Soviet forces often counted for little. For example, men of the 882nd Infantry Battalion of the Georgian Legion, on the night of 5 April 1945, rose against their captors on Texel, the largest of the islands to the north of the Netherlands, part of the German Atlantic Wall. The rising developed into a high-risk affair – not, as it was to turn out, from the forces of the Wehrmacht, but from the NKVD and NKGB. The Georgians had originally been captured on the Eastern Front and were offered by the Germans the choice of incarceration in a prison camp, which would have meant likely death, or enlisting in the German army. Calculating that the Allies would soon be landing, the Georgians, playing for time, had chosen the latter course. The Allies, however, had at that time other priorities than a relatively unimportant stretch of land.

Some 400 Germans, who had been sleeping in quarters shared with their Georgian allies, were knifed and bayoneted, and the violence spread across the island, involving guards and patrols on the roads. The Georgians ended up holding virtually the entire island, but could not maintain the position and German forces from the mainland wrested it back. The German commander of the 882nd battalion, Major Klaus Breitner, dismissed the insurgents as 'traitors and nothing else'. They were ordered to remove their uniforms, made to dig their own graves and were shot.

Predictably, those who somehow managed to survive faced more than four months of the standard post-repatriation 'processing' by the NKVD. The claim by many that they had only worn German uniforms to play for time while awaiting an Allied invasion was disregarded. Most of those who had been involved disappeared into the GULAG.

The power of SMERSH encroached still further. Its activities centred on the attitudes of young troops, who on discharge saw no reason to adhere to unquestioned loyalty and were apt to find themselves arraigned for 'systematic anti-Soviet talk and terroristic intentions'. There was a case of an NKVD rifle battalion chief of staff who had 'systematically carried out counter-revolutionary propaganda among the troops... and had slandered leaders of the Party and the Soviet government'. His penalty was eight years in the GULAG. SMERSH repression was also directed high up the ladder. Abakumov issued orders for the monitoring of the telephone calls of all senior generals and marshals. Even Zhukov was not immune.

Poland fighting on

The end of fighting in western Europe tended to distract attention from another ongoing conflict that showed little signs of abating. Within Poland, opposition to the communists by forces loyal to the AK was fierce and unrelenting, waged in the full knowledge that defeat would mean annihilation. Beria was well aware of Stalin's burning hatred of the Poles. On 17 May 1945 he reported to Stalin: 'Bands of Armia Krajowa bandits are continuing fighting in many parts of Poland, attacking prisons, militia headquarters, state

security departments, banks, businesses and democratic
organisations.' He backed up his claims by declaring that AK groups
and forces of the Ukrainian Patriotic Army were involved. The need
for action became steadily more urgent in the face of demands from
the communists in Poland for its rebels to be quelled. Here was an
obvious role for the NKVD.

Germany was no longer seen as a major problem by the NKVD,
particularly as its eastern sector was now under Soviet control. The
priority shifted to Poland. Fifteen NKVD regiments, in the charge
of General Nikolai Selivanovsky, Abakumov's deputy at SMERSH
and holding the added post of Councillor at the Polish Ministry of
Public Security, were despatched to police the Poles.

So the war's end brought little relief to the suffering of countless
Polish citizens in the hands of the NKVD. Wanda Krasnodebska, a
prisoner of the Germans after the Warsaw Rising, had managed to
make for Kutno, west of the capital, securing a cover job with the
Red Cross. But in fact she was working as a resistance courier,
despatching clandestine messages and spreading underground
literature as well as sheltering Poles on the run from the Nazis. At
the start of the war, her pilot husband, Zdzislaw, had flown to Britain
to serve with the Royal Air Force. It was a year before Wanda heard
his name and that of other pilots broadcast during a clandestine
radio despatch from London. At the war's end, the NKVD were
ready to pounce. A summons came from the local office of the
NKVD. Wanda's inquisitor demanded to know Zdzislaw
Krasnodebski's whereabouts. A photograph of him in his RAF
uniform was thrust at her, along with the accusation that both she
and her husband were British spies. She managed to keep her nerve,
replying: 'I wouldn't even know what a spy is supposed to do. I have
never been a spy and never met any spies.' The riposte was vintage
NKVD: 'It doesn't matter what spies do. What matters is what we
do with spies.'

She was subjected to round-the-clock surveillance. In the
meantime, thanks to a contact with the government-in-exile in
London, the Home Army learnt that her husband had been traced.
Wanda was eventually smuggled aboard a freight train to Warsaw,
from where she made her way to Krakow. Hiding with other

fugitives in the back of a truck, the party reached the Czech border, which was crossed after the payment of heavy bribes. Wanda's final destination was a Red Cross billet in British-occupied Germany and eventual reunion with her husband.

Although the fighting was finished, at the end of the war there were still Germans who were the butt of the NKVD's determination to seek out those it still regarded as enemies. In mid-1945, thirty-three youths aged between fifteen and twenty-one living in the east German state of Thuringia in the Soviet occupation zone were arrested, suspected of links with the Wehrwolves. Many of them faced long prison terms. One of those arrested was Helmut Braun, then sixteen, who recalled in 1993:

> I had been in a group photo of the Hitler Youth Fire Brigade which an informer had taken to the NKVD. One evening, I had gone out to call on my friend, Gunther Simm. As I was entering his house, a Red Army soldier was standing behind me. Pointing his machine pistol, he commanded: 'You are Helmut Braun. Come with me!' At the first interrogation, I had to tell my inquisitor my life story. Since I was just 16, it didn't take long. One of the interpreters shouted: 'You are Helmut Braun and you have forgotten you are a Wehrwolf'. Then came the first blow which knocked me out of the chair. A Russian Lieutenant and his interpreter were renowned for giving us prisoners a good kicking. They stamped on our faces and hands or kicked us in the stomach or testicles. Conditions were at their worst at the NKVD prison in Weimar. They said: 'It does not matter if you die. You Fascist, you Wehrwolf.'
>
> From the first day on, prisoners were not allowed to wash, or be let out into a yard for fresh air and exercise. They received no medical attention and their daily rations were a piece of wet bread and a small bowl of watery soup. There were lice, bedbugs and cockroaches in the cells. Many of those held were beaten, frozen or starved and each NKVD jail had an execution chamber in its cellars. When the guards hauled the youths out of their cells, they said: 'Don't worry, we are not going to shoot you.'

The methods used by the NKVD for interrogation had not changed. No rest was allowed during the day. Questioning started starting at around 21.00 hours and lasted well into the morning. The same questions were asked after gaps of several hours. This technique invariably produced different answers which were recorded as deliberate lies. Further beatings followed. One way of getting prisoners to sign incriminating confessions was to make them stand for several hours naked in a cage doused with cold water.

At the end of the war, after serving with the Wehrmacht, another victim was twenty-one-year-old Walter Jurss, who returned to Rostock on the Baltic Sea coast, a major industrial centre of the German Democratic Republic. He secured a clerical job in the port, which was closely patrolled by the Red Army.

> We were in charge of all the railway traffic. It was our job to route the trains with wagons onto the ships... Because of my job I knew the contents of every wagon.
>
> I therefore saw everything the occupying power 'exported' – plundered – via the port. It was simply everything that had not been nailed down and which was stolen for production or sale in the Soviet Union.

What he had witnessed, together with his links with student politics, brought him to the attention of the NKVD, who detained him for questioning.

> I was thrown into a room in the cellar, with just a wooden bed in it. No window, only a 100-watt light day and night. I was not allowed to lie down during the day and the interrogations nearly always started at 21.00 hours and went on until early morning. Records of the interrogations were always made in Russian and every page had to be signed. After a few days the female interpreter started kicking me on the shins and hitting me. One officer had a special method, he repeatedly hit me over the head with a ruler for a long time before saying casually: 'What is it they say in German, a few taps on the head increases the ability to think'. Headaches that lasted for days were the result. Food was one piece of bread and a bowl of soup...

After about three months I was transferred in handcuffs to the city of Schwerin in the north. After a period in solitary confinement I was moved to a double cell with twelve fellow prisoners. Interrogations were nearly always at night and always just before meal time, so that after the interrogation, at about 0400 hours in the morning, there was only cold water left. At first the interrogations took place every day, later one sometimes waited three to four weeks. The toilet was a cooking-pot or a bucket, and sometimes the lid did not fit properly. Once a female medical orderly came round with a tray, with a hot towel on it and a green cucumber cut into slices about 2cm thick and gave us each one piece saying: 'These are vitamins'.

Twenty-six-year-old electrical engineer Gunther Krause, a former tank commander from the city of Gera in Thuringia, endured imprisonment and privation until October 1950. He had been marked for arrest the moment he was released from being a prisoner of the Americans and predictably accused of having been an anti-communist spy during his wartime role as a member of the Hitler Jugend.

The Russians who arrested me were drunk and they gave me a good beating and broke my nose. The jail was a former police prison and I was thrown into a cell with four others. Towards morning I was woken by a terrible noise. Prisoners in the next cell, youths aged between 14 and 18, told me they had been sentenced to death. Clad only in their underclothes they were driven away and later shot in a remote spot.

Then there was transportation to the former concentration camp at Sachsenhausen, about 40 prisoners to each wagon and 200 prisoners all told. The guards were only happy when the doors of the wagons were closed and if this wasn't done quickly enough then they hit us with their rifle butts. No hygiene controls were carried out. We certainly had enough vermin, like bed bugs which tormented us the whole night long. We also had rats, which ran directly over our faces in the night and nibbled at the few possessions we had left. The death rate in the huts was extremely high. No day passed without two or three prisoners being carried out of the huts. The dead were only buried at night. Special teams of prisoners were selected for this task. The dead were buried either in the commander's yard or in the woods.

Uranium energy

John Cairncross, the British NKVD informant who worked for MI6 (UK Foreign Intelligence), had passed to Moscow details of British development of uranium atomic energy to produce explosive material. Soviet scientists began investigating ways of stealing a march on Britain in order to gain for the Soviet Union supremacy in the field of atomic weaponry.

Beria was put in charge of the entire atomic bomb project. Prisoners with specialist building skills were set to work, constructing laboratories and laying railway track. For scientists, the outcome could be grim. Many of those working at the Russian Federal Nuclear Centre (otherwise known as Arzamas-16) at Sarov, some 300 miles east of Moscow, suffered the effects of radiation sickness. It was to be August 1949 before the first Soviet bomb was tested in Kazakhstan.

By then the NKVD had undergone significant structural changes. In 1946 it was renamed MVD (*Ministerstvo Vnutrennikh Del*, Ministry of Internal Affairs) with most of its responsibilities passed to the MGB (*Ministerstvo Gosudarstvennoi Bezopasnosti*, Soviet Ministry of State Security). For Beria, it meant losing a grip on power, even though he was promoted to full membership of the Politburo, a move many saw as a conciliatory gesture, while others believed it be the first stage of his planned removal.

Stalin's memory loss, arteriosclerosis and fatigue made his suspicion of colleagues even more marked. His paranoia raged. Removals included Molotov, whom Stalin considered had abused his position by seeking popularity abroad. Vsevolod Merkulov, minister for state security, was accused of softness, and Abakumov, the self-indulgent, sadistic head of SMERSH, was condemned for corruption.

Stalin's death

Stalin's death on 5 March 1953, following collapse and coma, had succeeded a drunken dinner in the company of Beria, Malenkov, Nikita Khrushchev and Nikolai Bulganin, all of whom were contenders for the succession. Beria lost no time in moving to strengthen control of his security empire. His powers seemed enormous and unassailable. He commanded the political police, all external espionage, much of the militia, the labour camps and their inmates. He also had links with a substantial portion of Soviet industry. At the same time, there were signs of moves against him, prompted by his behaviour at the time of Stalin's death. Svetlana, Stalin's daughter, in a state of shock, described Beria as appearing 'radiant' and 'regenerated'. While the rest of those present at the death bed queued to kiss the still-warm corpse, Beria strode from the room and shouted to his chauffeur: 'Khrustalev, the car!' His destination had been the Kremlin.

Khrushchev, the arch plotter, set about scheming for Beria's downfall, summoning support from a sympathetic Zhukov. A bare month after Stalin's death, a useful pretext was provided by Beria's actions in the wake of a surge of unrest in East Berlin. Some 10,000 workers had erupted onto the streets, staging lightning strikes, calling for free elections and protesting at demands to increase production.

Blaming the crisis on the East German authorities and calling for a fundamental overhaul, Beria had pulled out some 800 members of the MVD, responsible for security at the behest of the NKVD. This proved a serious miscalculation. Sections of the Western press and the media were alerted to what were seen as weaknesses in Soviet security. Moreover, a source of particular anxiety to the Kremlin was the fear of unrest spreading to other communist satellites.

Khrushchev, however, recognised the danger of acting precipitously in case Beria succeeded in summoning support from his own security units. Thus, when he presided over a crucial Praesidium meeting, which an unsuspecting Beria attended, he did so with a gun bulging in his pocket. When Malenkov pressed a concealed alert button, Beria was seized by a group of armed officers, headed by Zhukov. His destination was a bunker beneath Osipenko Street in central Moscow with its 65 sq ft windowless cell, bare except for a wooden bed, two tables and a chair. The light was kept on at all times.

A deflated figure, stripped of all arrogance, Beria wrote a string of letters to his former colleagues, pleading for his life to be spared and begging them to find:

> ...the smallest job for me... You will see that in two or three years I'll have straightened out fine and will still be useful to you... I ask the comrades to forgive me for writing somewhat disjointedly and badly because of my condition, and also because of the poor lighting and not having my pince-nez.

At his trial he was found guilty of the blandly composed legal indictment: 'to revive capitalism and restore the rule of the bourgeoisie'. His execution, on 23 December 1953, was accompanied by total humiliation. He was stripped to his underwear, a towel stuffed into his mouth and a bandage wrapped round his face. General Batitsky, who had guarded Beria for six months, fired directly into his forehead and was later promoted to Marshal for his role. The body was cremated.

Beria, as a traitor, became a 'non-person'. 'Advice' was given to subscribers to the *Great Soviet Encyclopaedia* that Beria's entry should be replaced by an article on the Bering Sea. Instructions were issued to all government departments that portraits of Beria should be removed from the walls of their offices.

These events indicate that the baleful post-war hangover of Soviet tyranny continued long after the NKVD had effectively merged with the MVD, to become, after a number of name changes, the KGB (*Komitet Gosudarstvennoy Bezopasnosti*, Soviet Security and Intelligence Service), which in its turn was expunged during the decisive thawing, in the early 1980s, of the Cold War. Yet there remains a successor, FSB (*Federalnaya Sluzhba Bezopasnosti Rossiyskoy Federatsii*), which serves as a reminder that, much as Russian intelligence may have evolved since the collapse of the Soviet Union, it has yet to come to terms with its own past.

Select Bibliography

The author and publishers have made every effort to contact the copyright holders of material reproduced in this book, and wish to apologise to those they have been unable to trace.

Anders, Lt General Wladyslaw, *An Army In Exile*, Macmillan, 1949

Andreyev, Catherine, *Vlasov and the Russian Liberation Movement*, Cambridge University Press, 1987

Applebaum, Anne, *Gulag*, Allen Lane, The Penguin Press, 2003, pp 394–396

Beevor, Antony, *Stalingrad*, Penguin Books 1998. US: Penguin Puttnam Inc.

Beevor, Antony, *Berlin The Downfall 1945*, Viking, 2002.

Beevor, Antony and Vinogradova, Luba (Eds), *Writer At War: Valery Grossman with the Red Army 1941–45*, Vintage, 2006

Bellamy, Chris, *Absolute War: Soviet Russia in the Second World War*, Pan Macmillan, 2007

Biddiscombe, Perry, *Wehrwolf! The History of the National Socialist Guerilla Movement, 1944–1946*, University of Wales Press, Cardiff, 1998

Braithwaite, Rodric, *Moscow 1941: A city and its people at war*, Profile Books, 2006

Bullock, Alan, *Hitler and Stalin. Parallel Lives*, Harper Collins, 1991

Butler, Rupert, *Stalin's Instruments of Terror: CHEKA, OGPU, NKVD, KGB, FROM 1917 TO 1991*, Amber Books, 2006

Cross, Robin, *Fallen Eagle: The Last Days of the Third Reich*, Michael O'Mara Books Ltd, 1995

Davies, Norman, *Rising '44. The Battle For Warsaw*, Pan Books, 2004

Deschner, Gunther, *Heydrich: The Pursuit of Total Power*, Orbis Publishing, 1981

Ellis, Frank, *And Their Mothers Wept: The Great Fatherland War in Soviet and Post Soviet Russian Literature*, Heritage House Press, 2007

Foley, Charles *Commando Extraordinary*, Longmans, Green & Co., 1954

Foot, M.R.D., *SOE: An outline history of the Special Operations Executive 1940–46*, BBC, 1984

Garlinski, Josef, *Poland and the Second World War*, Macmillan, 1985

Hastings, Max, *Armageddon. The Battle For Germany 1944–45*, Macmillan, 2004

Hohne, Heinz, *Codeword: Direktor. The Story of the Red Orchestra*, Secker & Warburg, 1970

Infield, Glenn B., *Skorzeny: Hitler's Commando*, Military Heritage Press, 1981

Irving, David, *Uprising!*, Hodder & Stoughton, 1981

Jones, Michael K., *Leningrad State of Siege*, John Murray, 2008

Kapuscinski, Ryszard, *Imperium*, Granta Books, UK, 1994

Knight, Amy, *Beria, Stalin's First Lieutenant*, Princeton, NJ, 1993

Lucas, James, *War on the Eastern Front 1941–1945* Lucas, Macdonald & Jane's Publishing Group, 1980

Merridale, Catherine, *Ivan's War. The Red Army 1939–45*, Faber & Faber, 2005

O'Donnell, James P., *The Berlin Bunker*, J.M. Dent & Sons, 1979

Olson, Lynne and Cloud, Stanley, *For Your Freedom and Ours. Forgotten Heroes of World War Two*, William Heinemann, Random House, 2003

Overy, Richard, *Russia's War*, Penguin Books, 1997

Payne, Robert, *The Life and Death of Lenin*, Simon and Schuster, New York, 1964

Rayfield, Donald, *Stalin And His Hangmen*, Viking, 2004

Rees, Laurence, *World War 2: Behind Closed Doors*, Ebury Press, 2005

Rust, Gustav (Ed), *In the Clutches of the NKVD: Documentation from NKVD/Stasi Files*, Polit-Verlag Gustav Rusi, Berlin, 1999

Rzhevskaya, Elena, *Memoirs of a Wartime Interpreter*, Mouria Publishing House, Netherlands, by permission of ELKOST Literary Agency, 2009

Sakaida, Henry, *Heroes of the Soviet Union*, Osprey Publishing, 2004

Sebag Montefiore, Simon, *Young Stalin* Weidenfeld & Nicholson, 2007

Seth, Ronald, *The Executioners: The Story of SMERSH*, 1967
Solzhenitsyn, Aleksandr, *The Gulag Archipelago*, Harper Collins, 1995
Stephan, Robert W. *Stalin's Secret War. Soviet Counter Intelligence Against The Nazis*, University Press of Kansas, 2004
Sudoplatov, Pavel, and Sudoplatov, Anatoli, *Special Tasks: The Memoirs of An Unwanted Witness – A Soviet Spy Master*, Hachette Book Group, USA, 1994
Tolstoy, Nikolai, *Victim of Yalta*, Hodder & Stoughton, 1977
Trepper, Leopold, *The Great Game. Memoirs of a Master Spy*, Sphere Books Ltd, 1977
Volkogonov, Dimitri, *Trotsky, The Eternal Revolutionary*, Harper Collins, 1997
Walker, Jonathan, *Poland Alone: Britain, SOE and the Collapse of the Polish Resistance*, The History Press, 2008
Wittlin, Thaddeus, *Commissar: The Life and Death of Lavrenty Pavlovich Beria*, Angus & Robertson, 1973
Werth, Alexander, *Russia At War*, Pan Books Ltd, 1964

Index